Vijay Tendulkar, the Playwright

Vijay Tendulkar, the Playwright
Champion of Social Justice

Vani Devulapally

Prestige Books International
New Delhi

Published by
Prestige Books International
New Delhi 110 060
email: prestigebooks@gmail.com

Associate Office
P.O. Box 2250
Sydney, NSW 2001

ISBN: 978-93-82186-54-0

Printed in India

Contents

Dedicated

to

My Parents

Smt. Lakshmi

&

Sri Gopal Kishan Rao

whose love and support made me what I am today

There are times when one's life appears to be a stage—people come, people go—they come in order to go, and go with no intent of return; when they return, they return as one's past—a past that would make you feel the present is false.

Vijay Tendulkar

Acknowledgements

I owe deeply to all who have directly or indirectly contributed to the completion of this book, which is based on my Ph.D. thesis carried out at Kakatiya University, Warangal, Telangana. I gratefully acknowledge my gratitude to my research supervisor, Prof. M. Rajagopalachary, former Principal, University Arts & Science College, Kakatiya University, without whose guidance I could not have carried out this work. Prof. Chary was kind enough to spare considerable time at every stage of my study. Academic discussions with the faculty at the Department of English, Kakatiya University, Warangal, the English Foreign Language University, and Central University of Hyderabad, Hyderabad immensely enriched my work. I profusely thank them all.

I thank my beloved mother Smt. Lakshmi, for introducing me to the world of books; my father, Sri Gopal Kishan Rao, for his guidance. I am indebted to my brother-in-law, late Sri V. Keshava Rao for his motivation and encouragement and my sister, Smt. Vanaja, brothers, Dr. Praveen, Associate Professor of Anaesthesia, Kakatiya Medical College, Warangal, and Ramana, Senior Director, Infinite Computer Solutions, Maryland, USA, for their unconditional support and love. Also, I thank all the members of Devulapally and Manduva families for their moral support.

I thank my husband, Mr. M.V. Prabhakar Rao, Manager, Andhra Bank, Madikonda, Warangal, and my son, M. Sunnihith Bharadwaj, for their moral support and for enduring all the inconvenience with great understanding due to my involvement with research.

I express my gratitude to Dr. R.K. Dhawan and Dr. Suman Bala of the University of Delhi for their invaluable support and guidance in the preparation of this project. Finally, I thank Prestige Books International for bringing out this book so elegantly and expeditiously.

Vani Devulapally

Preface

Vijay Tendulkar (1928-2008) is a prolific Indian playwright. He is also a screen and television writer, literary essayist, political journalist and social commentator. He wrote fifty four plays in more than fifty years. With his great insights into human nature and human complexities as a responsible writer towards society, he raised the dignity of the modern Indian drama. He touched on each and every aspect of modern human society in general and Indian society in particular. He used naturalistic, realistic, expressionistic, humanistic and symbolic modes and made Marathi theatre avant-garde with his innovative experiments.

His achievement as a playwright is seen in his one-act plays as well as his full-length plays. Most of his plays have been regarded as Marathi theatre classics. His plays have been translated and performed in many Indian languages. By providing insight into major social events and political upheavals during his life, Tendulkar became one of the most powerful radical political voices in the Maharashtra of recent times.

Tendulkar won numerous awards from the Government of Maharashtra and from the Government of India for his outstanding contribution to the Indian drama. He received Maharashtra Gaurav Puraskar in 1999, the Sangeet Natak Akademi Award in 1970 and Akademi's highest award for "lifetime contribution" in 1998, and also the Sangeet Natak Akademi Fellowship (Ratna Sadasya). In 1984 he received Padmabhushan award from the Government of India for his literary accomplishments. In 1977, he won the National Film Award for Best Screen Play for his movie *Manthan*, directed by

Shyam Benegal. The latest recognition for life-time literary achievement was the Katha Chudamani award in 2001. Two national (1992 and 2005) and one international (held in New York in 2004) drama festivals of his plays were organized.

In all his plays Tendulkar explores the human predicament with authenticity. He observes: "The basic urge (to write) has always been to let out my concern vis-à-vis my reality; the human condition as I perceive it" (Banerjee 573). Tendulkar's plays are a product of his own observation and experiences. In an interview he remarks: "My work has come from within me, as an outcome of my observation of the world in which I live" (Tendulkar 72).

In Tendulkar's plays women play a principal role. His female characters are mainly drawn from the lower and middle classes: housewives, teachers, mistresses, daughters, film extras, slaves, servants etc. These women represent not only just a variety of social strata but also a broad range of emotions. His plays continue to be enigmatic, raising more questions than easy or comfortable answers. His body of work is endowed with an unusual subtlety that raises the plays above conventional social melodrama.

Chiefly, three dominant themes are found in Tendulkar's plays; power, violence and exploitation. His plays have been discussed in varying degrees, importantly from four angles; sociological, psychological, philosophical and theatrical. The quest of Tendulkar is to find the meaning of life in the need-based modern, materialistic life. He voices against loss of humanity, mechanical and materialistic nature of modern life, the impersonal and virulent social environment.

Though a number of critics have studied and discussed the themes of Tendulkar, the theme of social realism which he deals with in most of his major plays finds scant attention. The major thrust of Tendulkar's plays is, in fact, on social realism. Hence this study. Though Tendulkar's social realism can be seen in many of his plays, the study is limited to five of his major plays, namely, *Silence! The Court is in Session*, *Sakharam Binder*, *Ghashiram Kotwal*, *Kanyadaan* and *Kamala*. These plays are chosen for study because they represent different phases of Tendulkar's career and are the finest expression of his social realism. The present study is divided into seven chapters.

Chapter I broadly introduces Tendulkar's life and work in brief and the influences on him. It traces the origin and development of Indian drama from Bharata to the modern regional drama in translation. It gives an overview of Tendulkar's thematic complex art and vision. Tendulkar's concern is not about hypothetical pain or an imaginary world of sorrow. He is from a middle class family and he has seen the brutal ways of life by keeping his eyes open. His vision of life has come from within him as an outcome of his observation of the world in which he lives.

Chapter II is an analysis of *Silence! The Court is in Session* which reveals how gender inequalities make women insecure and how natural justice is denied to them in a male dominated society. The play also exposes not only the double standards of men but also the role of women in internalizing certain hypocritical values, subjugating and subordinating men. The play is considered a 'legal plea' which demands emancipation, equality and liberation of women and stresses the need for a social transformation of law, culture, and social pattern that chiefly mirrors the phallocentrism. *Silence! The Court is in Session* is the first significant modern Indian play in any language to center on woman as protagonist and victim. Leela Benare is school teacher, who is lively, independent, outspoken and assertive woman. She is a member of a drama company whose objective is to bring about a social change in the people through their performance. Benare's adoration for the intelligent professor Damle is exploited by him sexually, making her pregnant. He denies marrying her as he is already married and has children. Thus Benare becomes a prey for phallocentrism. In a seemingly mock-trial presented with great artistry by the dramatist, Benare is actually tried for her illicit relationship with Prof. Damle resulting in pregnancy. She is interrogated inhumanly and judged guilty in the male-centric society. At the end of her humiliation in the trial, the impression is given that it is all done only for fun.

Chapter III analyses *Sakharam Binder*. The play bluntly exposes the hypocrisy of our society in a realistic manner. It is a deft picturization of an egotistical man's struggle between two different women and exemplifies modern broken family system. Sakharam, a book-binder, does not believe in the institution of marriage and arranges for live-in relationships with single women. His relationship with Laxmi shows tendencies of being religious and domesticated. After Champa's arrival to his house, he is transformed into a sensuous, lewd, drunkard with thoughts only of sexual enjoyment. But he comes to know that Champa also develops illicit contact with Dawood, his friend. Unable to bear this, his masculinity is badly hurt. Hence, in his anger, he kills Champa. However, the play exposes the greater hypocrisy in man-woman relationships in the matrix of the institution of marriage which poses a threat to the institution.

Chapter IV analyses *Kanyadaan* which deals with the sensitive issue of inter-caste marriage in a caste-based society. It is the story of a Brahmin girl who marries a dalit boy under the influence of her father's ideological dream for a casteless society. Ideology and politics are two different aspects to mix with in modern political scenario. Tendulkar has tried to criticize the same in this play. The play also exposes the nature of human complexities, its violence, human naiveté and hypocrisies which lead to incompatible bonding with unmitigated suffering at interpersonal level. Nath and Seva are couple as well as social workers, who confront with an intriguing situation when their own daughter, Jyoti expresses her desire of marrying a dalit boy, Arun, who is a poet. It is a test for their ideology now. Nath reacts ecstatically to the decision of his daughter, but, Seva, somehow, does not like this proposal after she has come to know about the boy's family background, his educational qualification, and employment. Despite her reluctance, the marriage between Jyoti and Arun takes place. But the marriage becomes sour and the husband turns violent towards his wife. Unable to bear the torture, Jyoti goes to her parents, but later realizes that her place is with her husband. She realizes that Arun writes good poetry, but as a man he is worse. She accepts this crisis as a sordid reality and goes back to Arun, leaving her parents forever. The terrible truth in Tendulkar's play is about the violence between dalit husbands and the Brahmin or upper caste wives.

Chapter V is a critique of *Ghashiram Kotwal* which deals with the story of an ordinary, simple Brahmin from Kanauj. He comes to Pune to try his luck. He is jilted, hurt, humiliated and victimized. Waiting for revenge, he uses his daughter Gauri to secure him the significant and powerful position of Kotwal. Ghashiram, becoming Kotwal of Pune, avenges his insult and punishes the whole city. The victim turns victimizer which is a theme of great interest to Tendulkar. The play is based on certain episodes in the life of Nana Phadnavis, one of the major architects of Peshwa supremacy during the decline of Maratha Empire. Tendulkar portrays him as a leader with an overpowering weakness for young Brahmin girls of Puna. To get Kotwalship of Puna, Ghashiram offers his young and innocent daughter Lalita Gauri to Nana. But, after losing interest Nana gets rid of her. Actually Nana uses Ghashiram as a weapon to keep the Brahmins of the city of Puna under check. When Ghashiram becomes the worst foe of city Brahmins, the latter unite with the demand of killing of Ghashiram, resulting in pathetic ending of his life.

Chapter VI interprets *Kamala*, a story of a sensational journalist Jaisingh Jadhav who buys an innocent woman Kamala in a flesh market and presents her in a press conference to prove the existence of flesh trade. It also presents the suppression of an educated woman Sarita who realizes her position later through Kamala. It also exposes the negligible value of woman as a commodity in the modern globalized world. In a country like India there is no difference between a tribal woman and an educated woman: both are suppressed in a male-chauvinistic society.

Jaisingh is self-centred and egotist. He appears to have a great concern for the maladies of society. But his hypocrisy is seen when he presents Kamala in her torn clothes at the press conference. He has done this for sensationalism and for name and fame. His wife Sarita, though educated, is helpless in averting this. But soon she realizes her place in the family. She strongly opposes the chauvinism shown by her husband and decides to leave him. But due to some reasons Sarita resolves to give moral support to her husband in the crisis and continue not as a puppet in his hands but as a human being. The play ends with this optimistic note.

Chapter VII presents the conclusion of the study. As a keen observer of human nature, Tendulkar visualizes social problems and depicts them in his plays of great relevance even today. His endeavour to explore humanism, re-presenting it in his work will be remembered. The study reveals Tendulkar as a promising playwright who influenced and inspired the contemporary Marathi drama. He seems to suggest that man has to ultimately face the reality, however, harsh and dark it may be. Though Tendulkar's world appears to be pessimistic and tragic it is not devoid of hope. It suggests the need to accept life as it comes one's way. Life is a gift. We need to receive it and utilize it in a proper way. Life is a challenge and we need to face it accordingly. Problems and sufferings are part and parcel of human life. When man realizes this truth and learns to face it, nothing bothers him. When life becomes a conflict, we need to fight it through till we get justice; then only it raises our dignity as human beings. Tendulkar passed away on 19th May 2008 leaving an indelible mark of his own on the world of Indian drama.

Contexts of Indian Drama

Of all the three forms of literature namely poetry, drama and novel, drama is the most complex in terms of its creation and reception. It is still alive despite its several limitations. Like poetry, the popularity of drama too has declined in recent times, for, the modern man has little time to spare to read and comprehend drama. It can be said that drama is the art of necessity; it is of a necessity to serve social purpose as it is more effective medium of communication than other two forms, poetry and novel.

Drama has many similarities with novel; both novel and drama are made up of the same elements such as plot, characters, dialogue, milieu, setting and theme. "The general principles of criticism which we have laid down for the study of plot, characterization, dialogue, local and temporal setting, and interpretation of life, in prose fiction, for the most part, as will be seen in respect of the same constituents in a play" (Hudson 171). Though the elements of drama and novel are identical, the novelist and the dramatist will have to work under conditions of vast dissimilarity owing to the circumstances existing during the days of their composition. As a result, the principles of dramatic composition and the laws of its technique keep changing as per the requirements of the dramatist.

The structural features of the drama in modern times need to be examined and studied as they are different, compared to those of the epic and novel:

> The ancient epic was composed for recitation; the modern novel is written to be read; the drama is designed for representation by actors who impersonate the characters of its story and among whom the narrative and the dialogue are distributed. While the epic

> and the novel relate and report, the drama imitates by action and speech. (Hudson 172-73)

While the novel is self-contained and can be read and enjoyed, the same is not the case with the drama. Whatever be the changes it has undergone, drama continues to be associated with the stage as it is called a stage-play. The continuance of drama as a unique form of art transcends the barriers of region, religion, nationality and language.

Drama, in India owes its origin way to the *Natya Sastra,* the oldest of the texts of the theory of the drama. We find references to drama in Patanjali's *Vyakarana Mahabhyasa,* Vatsyayana's *Kamasutra,* Kautilya's *Arthasastra* and Panini's *Ashtadhyayi.* Thus the origin of Sanskrit drama goes back to 1000 B.C. Sanskrit literature is divided into two types, Drishya and Sravya: that which can be seen on being exhibited and that which can be heard on being recited. The first one is called 'drama' and the second one 'poetry.' Drama in Sanskrit literature is covered under the broad umbrella of 'Rupaka' which means depiction of life in various aspects represented in forms by actors who assume various roles.

Nataka is one of the ten classifications of 'Rupaka' which contains all dramatic presentations. The Sanskrit drama thrives on three basic ingredients such as Plot (Vastu), Hero (Neta) and Sentiment (Rasa). The plot could be either principal (adhikarika) or accessory (prasangika). The former concerns the primary characters of the theme and pervades the entire play. The latter serves to further and supplement the main topic and relates to subordinate characters other than the chief ones.

Bharata's *Natya Sastra,* the most significant work on Indian drama, dealt with composition, production, and stage equipment including music. Bharata's work was recognized as the 'fifth Veda.'

During the ancient times among the most celebrated dramatists are Ashwaghosh, Bhasa, Shudraka, Kalidas, Harsha,

Bhavabhuti, Vishakhadatta, Bhattanarayana, Murari and Rajesh Khora. These playwrights enriched Indian drama throughout their works like *Madhya-Mayyaayoda, Urubhangam, Karnabharam, Mrichkatikam, Abhigyana Sakuntalam, Malankagnimitram, Uttararamacharitam, Mudrarakshasa, Bhagavadajjukam, Matta Vilasa,* etc.

The chief contribution in the field of Indian drama is the contribution made by Kalidas, who is regarded as the Shakespeare of India. The Sanskrit drama reached its zenith during the 12th century in India and continued its sway till the Islamic invasion shifted the Sanskrit stage. However, Sanskrit plays were staged in Tamilnadu, Kerala, Karnataka, Andhra Pradesh, Uttara Pradesh and Maharashtra.

Though drama ceased to exist till the 16th century, it continued in one form or the other in all states during the 17th century. Thus we can find the beginnings of the people's theatre in diverse forms in these states. In Bengal it has appeared in the form of Yatra Kirtaniya, Paol and Gaon, in Madhya Pradesh it has taken the shape of Mach, in Kashmir it has assumed the guise of Bhandyathar. It was Bhavai and Ramleela in Uttar Pradesh. They were Nartana, Bhand, Ramleela and Rasleela in Maharashtra. In Rajasthan they were Tamasha, Raas and Jhoomer, in Punjab they were in the form of Bhangra and Giddha. In Assam it was Ahiyamat and Ankinatya, in Bihar they were Videshiya and Chaan while it was Kuchipudi in Andhra Pradesh.

During the 18th century Indian drama reached greater heights under the influence of western civilization on Indian life. Drama troupes from England and Italy toured India and staged several English plays, Shakespeare's in particular, in cities like Mumbai and Chennai. But the real beginning was in 1831 when Prasanna Kumar Thakur established "Hindu Rangamanch" in Kolkata and staged Wilson's English translation of Bhavabhooti's Sanskrit drama *Uttararamacharitam,* social drama of Girish Chand Ghosh, historical dramas of D.L. Roy and artistic dramas of Rabindranath Tagore, *Muktadhara, Chandalika* and *Chitra* continued to reach up to the stage of realistic dramas during the period of the worst ever famines of Bengal and the second world war.

While Bharatendu Harishchandra who was the father of Hindi drama developed amateur theatre, Postagipharmaji established the Parsi theatre during the year 1852. During the evolution of the Parsi theatre several new plays were performed on the stage paving a way for many such plays to be staged subsequently.

After a long hiatus of a few decades it was only by the early 20th century that "Indian English drama gathered momentum under the influence of British Drama. The pre-independence era saw some stalwarts like Rabindranath Tagore, Sri Aurobindo, T.P. Kailasam, A.S.P. Ayyar, Lobo-Prabhu, Harindranath Chattopadhyaya, Bharati Sarabhai, who contributed substantially to the evolution and development of Indian English drama" (Shukla 4).

The contribution made by Madhusudan Dutt, Sri Aurobindo and Rabindranath Tagore to the drama deserves a particular mention. Dutt's *Is this called Civilization?,* Tagore's plays, *The Post Office, Sacrifice, Red Oleanders, Chandalika, Natirpuja, The King of the Dark Chamber, The Cycle of Spring, Sanyasi* and *The Mother's Prayer*, originally written in Bengali, were translated into English. These plays are firmly rooted in the Indian ethos and ethics in their themes, characters and treatment.

Sri Aurobindo wrote five plays in blank verse, *Perseus the Deliverer, Vasavadatta, Radoguna, The Vizier's of Bassora* and *Eric*. The notable feature of Sri Aurobindo's plays is that they depict different cultures and countries in different epochs bringing with variety of characters, moods and sentiments.

Modern drama during the latter part of the 20th century which deviated from the classical and European models took its strong roots in history, legends, myth, religion and folklore in context with contemporary social, political and economic issues.

A cumulative theoretical tradition evolved by Mohan Rakesh, Badal Sircar, Vijay Tendulkar and Girish Karnad prepared the background for contemporary Indian English theatre.

Mohan Rakesh was one of those rare literary personalities who never accepted the traditional set up but always aspired to find and project something which is challenging and new. "Rakesh was a pioneer in more than one field of creative writing. In the field of the short story he initiated the "new story movement" in Hindi. In his novels and travelogues he explored the vast expanse of man's inner and outer world. And in the field of drama, he opened up new vistas by his untiring efforts." (Dass 7). He projected modern man's failure to understand himself or to understand the other, which is the real tragedy of modern life. This breakdown of communication is handled by Rakesh with a concentration, intensity and subtlety, rare in the earlier Hindi drama. *Ashadh Ka Ek Din* (*One Day in Ashadha*), *The Great Swans of the Waves, Half-Way House, Sipahi Ki Maa* (*A Soldier's Mother*) are some of his popular plays.

While Rakesh uses historical characters to project this breakdown of communication, Badal Sircar, the great Bengali playwright, uses contemporary situations and social problems to project the life-in-death attitude of modern life. The drama of 1880s bears testimony to this attitude of the middle classes towards social responsibility.

Sircar's "Third Theatre" has emerged out of his experiences both in India and abroad. In an interview Sircar once said that he makes use of whatever good he finds in any theatre. Sircar's "Third Theatre" is an outcome of a thriving process that has brought him and his theatre on to a new threshold. The first theatre—the city theatre is a commercial theatre, which exploits the people's imagination and participation for the sake of money. The Second Theatre, the indigenous folk theatre, is performed in the open and the audience is not expected to pay anything to watch these plays. So Sircar formulated his Third Theatre taking the best from both. He performs his production anywhere. And it is free. Defending his advocacy of free theatre, Sircar says, "We consequently proved that free theatre is an economically feasible proposition for any theatre group which does not have to pay its artists, as is mostly the case in India, particularly in West Bengal" (75). Sircar's Third Theatre is 'poor' because it does not have any external trappings like sets, lights, costumes, sound and make-up which are necessary in a commercial theatre. Based on the concepts of "Third Theatre," Sircar has produced several plays which include *Spartacus, Micchil* (*Procession*), *Bhoma* and *Basi Khabar* (*Stale News*). His famous plays are *Evam Indrajit, Baki Itihas* and *Shesh Nei* (*There's No End*).

If we consider Girish Karnad's contribution to Indian drama we realize how he, as a writer, director and actor, has substantially contributed to mould the tradition of Indian English Theatre. His dramatic sensibility was moulded under the influence of touring Natak companies and especially Yakshagana which was in those days not accepted as the purified art form. *Yayati* (1961), *Tughlaq* (1962), *Hayavadana* (1970) and *Nagamandala* (1972) are his well-known plays. He borrowed his plots from history, mythology, and old legends, but with intricate symbolism he tried to establish their relevance to contemporary socio-political conditions.

Mahesh Dattani, another major contemporary playwright, is regarded by *The International Herald Tribune* as "one of India's best and most serious contemporary playwrights writing in English." His plays are rooted in contemporary urban experience. He has the unique capacity to read the rumblings of contemporary urban Indian society and smell the perennial clash between tradition and modernity. He writes frankly about the oppressed or the marginalized class such as minorities, women, gays, hijras etc. Dattani's plays reveal the physical and spatial awareness of Indian theatre on the one hand and the textual rigour of Ibsen and Tennessee Williams on the other. Theatre is Dattani's life-long passion. His first play *Where There's a Will* was published in 1986 and since 1995 he has been devoting himself completely to the theatrical activities. For the first time in our country in 1998 Dattani set up his own theatre studio meant for the training of new talents in acting, directing and stage writing. In the same year he became the first Indian playwright to receive the prestigious Sahitya Akademi Award for his collection *Final Solutions* and *Other Plays*. Some of his other famous plays are *Seven Steps around the Fire, On a Muggy Night at Mumbai, Do the Needful, Bravely Fought the Queen, Tara, Dance like a Man.*

Manjula Padmanabhan is a powerful playwright and a cartoonist. Her play *Harvest* won the Onassis International Cultural Competitions Prize for theatrical plays in 1997 in Greece. Another play is *Lights Out*, in which she unveils the other side of Indian woman and her suffering. In the play the heart-rending screams of a woman which destroy the fabric of domesticity of a middle-class couple is noticeable. In her plays violence of women in many aspects of their daily life not only physical but more often mental and emotional is portrayed. Dina Mehta's first full-length play *The Myth Makers* won an award from Sultan Padamsee Playwrighting Competition in 1968, and *Tiger, Tiger* (a play on Tipu Sultan) in 1978 *Brides Are Not for Burning* (a play on dowry deaths) won the first prize in the worldwide competition sponsored by B.B.C. in 1979. Her other famous plays include *Getting Away with Murder, One Plus One Makes Nine* and *Sister like You.*

Sengupta is a columnist, poet, children's fiction writer and a playwright. Her first full-length play *Mangalam* won the award for its society-relevant theme in *The Hindu*. Her latest play *Keats* was shortlisted for the 1996 British Council International Playwriting Award and received a special commendation. Her play *Mangalam* reveals how women have been facing various kinds of violence and abuses for generations, even in the modern society.

Thus the world of modern Indian playwrights deals with the aspirations of the deprived and marginalized sections of society and delineates the burning conflicts of contemporary life. It is a blend of Western intellectual consciousness and Indian theatrical techniques. Hence their plays are considered experimental plays in modern Indian drama. These playwrights' interaction with the world theatre has broken our alienation from the rest of the world.

II

The name of Vijay Tendulkar is a by-word in Indian drama in general and in Marathi Theatre in particular. He was a versatile genius. He was an eminent Indian playwright, movie and television writer, literary essayist, political journalist, eloquent speaker and social commentator in Marathi and English. Many of his plays owed their inspiration to real life incidents and social upheavals throwing more light on harsh realities of life. Tendulkar's greatness as a teacher lies in the fact that he provided his guidance to students pursuing a course in play-writing in American universities. For more than fifty years Tendulkar had been a dominant influential dramatic personality in Maharashtra.

Tendulkar won numerous awards from the Government of Maharashtra and from the Government of India for his outstanding contribution to the Indian drama. He received Maharashtra State Government awards in 1956, 1961 and in 1972. He received Maharashtra Gaurav Puraskar in 1999. He achieved the Sangeet Natak Akademi Award in 1970 and Akademi's highest award for "life time contribution" in 1998, and the Sangeet Natak Akademi Fellowship (Ratna Sadasya). In 1984 he received Padmabhushan award from the Government of India for his literary accomplishments.

Tendulkar won the National Film Award for Best Screen Play for his movie *Manthan* directed by Shyam Benegal in 1977; Sangeet Natak Akademi Award & Kamaladevi Chattopadhyay Award for *Silence! The Court is in Session* in 1970. Filmfare Best Screen Play Award for *Akrosh* in 1981,

Padma Bhushan in 1984, Saraswati Samman in 1993, Sangeet Natak Akademi Fellowship in 1998, Kalidas Samman in 1999, Katha Chudamani Award in 2001 and The Little Magazine SALAM Award in 2006.

Vijay Dhondopant Tendulkar was born on 8 January 1928 in a Bhalavalikar Saraswat Brahmin family in Kolhapur, Maharashtra. His father was a clerk who also ran a small publishing business. The literary environment prevailing at home prompted Tendulkar to take to writing. He wrote his first story when he was only six years old. Vijay Tendulkar grew up watching western plays on account of which he felt inspired to write plays himself. When he was hardly eleven years old, he wrote and directed his first play in which he also acted. He left his studies at the age of 14 and took part in Indian Freedom Movement in 1942. His discontinuance of studies isolated him from his family and friends. Then writing became his immediate outlet. Yet most of his early writings were of a personal nature and not intended for publication.

Tendulkar began his career as a writer contributing articles for newspapers. He wrote his first play *Who Will Love Us?* at the age of fourteen. In his early 20s, he wrote another play *The Householder* which did not receive much recognition from the audience. As a result, he swore that he would never write again. However, in 1956, he broke his vow and wrote the next play *Shrimant* which established him as a good writer. *Shrimant* moved the conservative audience of the times with a story radical in nature wherein an unmarried young woman decides to keep her unborn child while her rich father tries to buy her a husband in an attempt to protect his social prestige.

Tendulkar's early struggle for survival and living for some time in huts in Mumbai provided him first-hand experience about the life of urban lower middle class. Thus he gave a new authenticity to their depiction in Marathi theatre.

Tendulkar's writings rapidly changed the story line of the modern Marathi theatre during the 1950s and 1960s with experimental presentation by theatre groups like "Rangayan." In these theatre groups the actors like Shri Ram Lagoo, Mohan Agashe and Subhas Deshpande gave new authenticity and power to Tendulkar's stories while introducing new sensibilities in Marathi theatre.

Tendulkar wrote the play *The Vultures* in 1961, but it was not produced until 1970. The story of the play was set in a morally collapsed family structure in which he explored the theme of violence. In his subsequent dramatic creations, Tendulkar explored violence in its various forms; domestic, sexual, communal and political. Thus *The Vultures* proved to be a turning point in Tendulkar's writings with regard to establishment of his own unique writing style.

Based on Fredrich Durrenmatt's short story *Traps* published in 1956, Tendulkar wrote the play *Silence! The Court is in Session.* It was staged for the first time in 1967 and proved one of his finest dramatic works. Satyadev Dubey made it a movie in 1971 and Tendulkar wrote its screen play. In his writing career stretching over more than five decades, Tendulkar wrote 30 full-length plays and 24 one act plays. Most of his plays have been regarded as Marathi theatre classics. His plays were translated and performed in many Indian languages.

The plays and other works of Tendulkar that established him as a prolific writer include *Householder* (1947), *The Rich* (1956), *An Island named Man* (1958), *Thief! Police!* (1959), *Bale Miltat* (1960), *The Vultures* (1961), *Marriage of a Village Mayor's Daughter* (1965), *Silence! The Court is in Session* (1967), *A Boa Constructor and Gandharwa* (1971), *Sakharam, the Book-Binder* (1972), *Kamala* (1981), *Madi* (*in Hindi*) (1982), *Kanyadaan* (*Giving away of a Daughter in Marriage*) (1983), *Agni, Encounter in Umbugland, Thus arrive the Birds, Kuttee, The Cyclist* (1991), *The Masseur* (2001), *It Has to be in One's Blood, Ask a Fakir's Lineage, My Sister, "Infinite" Turned "Hanumanta," Side Walk Emperor, A Friend's Story* (2001), *A play based on a novel by D.B. Mokashi, Balu Murar Rao,*

Bhalyakaka, I won I lost, His Fifth Woman (*in English*) (2004), *Baby* (1975), *Ghashiram, the Constable* (1972). The novels are: *Kadambari Part I* (1996), *Kadambari Part II* (2005). The short story anthologies are *Duel* (1961), *Butterflies* (1970). The translations are Mohan Rakesh's *Adhe Adhure* (originally in Hindi), Girish Karnad's *Tughlaq* (originally in Kannada), Tennessee Williams' *A Street Car named Desire* (originally in English). The Screen Plays are *Silence! The Court is in Session* (1972), *End of Night* (1975), *Confrontation* (1975), *Churning* (1976), *Throne* (1979), *The Depth* (1980), *Cry of the Wounded* (1980), *Unimaginable* (1981), *The Threshold* (1981), *Ardh Satya* (*Half Truth*) (1983), *Kamala* (1984), *Sardar* (1993), *Yeh Hai Chakkad Bakkad Bumbe Bo* (2003), *Eashwar Mime Co.* (The Mime Players) (2005). The dialogues are *Arvind Desai Ki Ajeeb Dastaan* (1978), 22 June 1987.

When social realism has become a strong force in dramatic creations, contemporary playwrights were cautiously exploring its limits. But, Tendulkar, embraced political radicalism, and courageously exposed political hegemony of the powerful and the hypocrisies of the Indian social mindset. Tendulkar's powerful expression of human anger has resulted in his receiving simultaneously both wide acclaim and high censure from the orthodox Brahmins and political heavy-weights.

By providing insight into major social events and political upheavals during his life, Tendulkar became one of the most powerful radical political voices in Maharashtra in recent times. Tendulkar was among the handful of playwrights along with Girish Karnad, Habib Tanvir and Badal Sircar who gave a new dimension to the content and form of Indian drama. He wrote about contemporary issues and themes in a unique way.

Tendulkar's writing of the screen-plays for the movies *Nishant* in 1974, *Akrosh* (*The Cry*) in 1980 and *Ardh Satya* (*Half Truth*) in 1984 established him as an important chronicler of violence of the contemporary period. He has written screen-plays for eleven movies in Hindi and for eight movies in

Marathi. His screen-plays for Marathi movies include *Samna* (*Confrontation*) in 1975, *Simhasan* (*Throne*) in 1979 and *Umbartha* (*The Threshold*) in 1981. The last movie is based on women's activism in India. It was directed by Jabbar Patel while Smita Patil and Girish Karnad played the lead roles.

During 1991 Tendulkar wrote a metaphorical play, *Safar* and *The Masseur* in 2001. Next he wrote two novels *Kadambari Ek* and *Kadambari Do* which dealt with sexual fantasies of an ageing man. In 2004, he wrote a one-act play *His Fifth Woman* which was his only first play in English. It was a sequel to his earlier exploration of the plight of women in *Sakharam Binder*. This play was first performed at the Vijay Tendulkar Festival in New York in October, 2004. During the 1990s Tendulkar wrote a well-received T.V. Serial *Swayamsiddha* in which his daughter Priya Tendulkar performed the main role.

Tendulkar's art lies in the fact that Tendulkar did not limit his art to writing plays alone. He wrote short-stories, novels and political articles in newspapers besides plays. Above all his art extends itself to acting, directing, screen-play writing. Tendulkar himself explains his multifaceted approach to art:

> I was a writer first and a playwright afterwards. Means I did not at any stage limit myself to playwriting but wrote—and loved to write—for different medium including the day-to-day newspaper journalism. While having to write for these medium I learnt to mould my language according to the requirements of the writing. This amounted to playing roles. In the morning I was a short story writer; during the day I had to write as a journalist; at night till morning I turned myself into a playwright. Therefore I did not develop one single rigid mould of writing style but enjoyed changing my roles and accordingly, my style. The journalist while writing an editorial had to call himself 'WE' and write with a certain force, finality and authority. A short story writer had to be introspective, had to have a sensitive eye for details and an objective, analytical mind. A playwright was required to be behind the curtain leaving the stage of his writing to his characters whom he would control—but from behind the curtain and indirectly. The

> characters would speak their minds and would have their own expression. (I)

Tendulkar died in Poona on 19 May 2008 fighting against the adverse effects of 'myasthenia gravis.' He experienced tragedy after tragedy before his death. Tendulkar's son, Raja and wife Nirmala died in 2001. His daughter Priya Tendulkar died the next year in 2002 of cancer.

Throughout his artistic career Tendulkar continued to receive both bouquets and brickbats for his plays depicting social realism. His social realism can be fully found in the portrayal of the themes of sex and violence. His first plays *Grihast* and *Shrimant* received acclaim. In his heyday, from the late 1960s to the mid-1980s, he received more brickbats. His plays such as *Gidhade* in 1970, *Sakharam Binder* and *Ghashiram Kotwal* in 1972 offended the self-proclaimed moralists and Brahmins who considered him a playwright with subversive ideas. False notions of morality received a beating in his writings which exposed middle class hypocrisy in a clinical and naturalistic manner, which was something that no other playwright had ever attempted before Tendulkar did.

In all his plays Tendulkar dealt with themes that unveil the exploitation of power and potent violence in human relationships. In this connection Tendulkar observes: "The basic urge (to write) has always been to let out my concern vis-à-vis my reality; the human condition as I perceive it" (Banerjee 573). Tendulkar presents his themes through all his plays from his own observation and experiences. In an interview Tendulkar once said:

> I have not written about hypothetical pain or created an imaginary world of sorrow. I am from a middle class family and I have seen the brutal ways of life by keeping my eyes open. My work has come from within me, as an outcome of my observation of the world in which I live. If they want to entertain and make merry, fine go ahead, but I can't do it, I have to speak the truth. (72)

In Tendulkar's plays women play a principal role. His female characters are mainly drawn from the lower and middle classes: housewives, teachers, mistresses, daughters, film extras, slaves, servants etc. These women represent not only just variety of social strata but also a broad range of emotions in his plays. They come from "the unbelievably gullible to the clever, from the malleable to the stubborn, from the conservative to the rebellious, from the self-sacrificing to the grasping." (Gokhale 32)

Tendulkar's characters are often composite reflection of contradictory personalities. They struggle between espoused values and conflicting actions. They seek independence, yet submissively struggle between physical desires and conscience. Tendulkar sought to minimize his personal influence on these characters and their personality development. He says, "They are in the play with their own minds, ways and destiny." (xxi)

Arundhati Banerjee in her "Introduction" to *Five Plays* by Vijay Tendulkar observes: "none of his creations are ever simplistic—like his genius they too have the same prismatic quality of giving forth new meanings as one turns them around in the light of one's understanding" (584). As a result, his plays continue to be enigmatic, raising more questions than easy or comfortable answers. His body of work is endowed with an unusual subtlety that raises the plays above hackneyed social melodrama.

While considering the thematic overview of Vijay Tendulkar's plays, we have to take the playwright's deep concern for human life and society of which he is an integral part. The result is that he continues to be in limelight with one controversy or the other surrounding him. In this context, Balwant Bhaneja in his article "Vijay Tendulkar (1928-2008)" writes:

> The inner core of Tendulkar's works is rooted in his deep comparison and respect for human life—for the life in the social

> reality in postcolonial India. Seeing its exploitation and waste, his response was an unrelenting literary output and non-stop social activism. Until his death, he was involved in cases, fiercely seeking justice for the victimized—mainly the poor and those disfranchised by communal riots and structural violence. Unlike the makers of the confrontational theatre of the late 1980s, he did not believe that "an evening at the theatre would change the society, but he was always hopeful that a good play could raise public awareness." (web)

Tendulkar took his role as a playwright to be a wonderful opportunity to highlight the issues, social, political and communal engaging his opponents in continuous public debate. There is rarely a play by Tendulkar which has not raised a controversy. This has resulted in numerous calls for banning his plays. It is surprising that most of these calls have not come from the authorities but from particular sections of society. For, they saw the attacks of the playwright on their power positions in politics, challenges to caste, gender or class structures.

Tendulkar's most popular play *Ghashiram Kotwal* had raised such a controversy when it was staged in 1972. It was stopped because the right wing nationalist RSS found it "anti-Brahmin" and charged that the negative depiction of the noble character of Nana Phadnavis was historically inaccurate. Defending the play, Tendulkar pointed out that *Ghashiram Kotwal* was not a historical play. He says:

> It is a story, in prose, verse, music and dance set in a historical era. Ghashirams are creations of socio-political forces which know no barriers of time and place. Although based on historical legend, I have no intention of commenting on the morals or lack of them, of the Peshwa Nana Phadnavis or Ghashiram. The moral of the story, if there is any, may be looked elsewhere (ix).

During 1980 before the play was performed at the Berlin International Theatre Festival, similar objections by way of protests were repeated prior to the troupe's departure from India. The right wing Shiv Sena Party approached the court to get a stay order against the impending international tour. The artists had to seek police protection. The court issued an order whereby it would be required that before each performance a statement approved by the court had to be read out. This statement publicly praised the achievements of Nana Phadnavis declaring that the play was not based on true history. The troupe followed the court order. The play had a successful tour of Western Europe with more than twenty-five performances. It received positive and enthusiastic reviews in the *London Times*, *the Guardian Derspeigel* and *New Theater Quarterly*.

Vijay Tendulkar's works present an interesting blend of content and structure. In his plays, he has experimented with every form, from traditional folk techniques in *Ghashiram Kotwal* with fifty characters dancing on the stage, to the minimalist Becketian bicyclist journey in *Safar* (*Cycle Wallah*) in 1993 and *The Masseur* in 2003, a full-length one character play with a bench as the only setting, to his last play, *His Fifth Woman* in 2004, a play, in which the two main characters wait outside a hospital with woman's body in a hand cart. Tendulkar always maintained that the structure of his plays was driven by the characters. It is this uniqueness that brings out their broad thematic impact. *Silence! The Court is in Session*, *Ghashiram Kotwal*, *Sakharam Binder* are recognized as his outstanding plays for their bold social themes and structured characterization. In *Safar* and *His Fifth Woman*, he dealt with the difficult themes about the meaning of life without straining to be philosophical or profound. These two plays have an unusual light touch despite their heavy themes. A trio of his plays, *Baby* in 1975, *Kamala* in 1982 and *Kanyadaan* in 1983 deal with insightful studies of women, developed as conventional three-act social dramas with his characteristically penetrating dialogue and characterization.

When we look at the plays of Vijay Tendulkar in relation to their thematic overview, we can find three dominant themes in them; power, violence and exploitation. The theme of power stretches itself to the power of politics, the power of wealth, the power of caste, the power of religion, the power of orthodoxy, the power of individual and above all the power of male dominance against women.

Violence is an integral part of social order and it cannot be isolated from the life of an individual and of society. Tendulkar believes that every individual must accept violence as a sordid reality from which one cannot escape nor one can avoid it. There may be individual violence as we find in *Sakharam Binder* or group violence as we see in *Ghashiram Kotwal.*

When it comes to the theme of exploitation, the exploitation appears in diverse forms in different degrees. There is exploitation of women by men, of the poor by the rich, of the ruled by the rulers. Michel Foucault defines Power "as the relationship in which one wishes to direct the behaviour of another." Samik Bandyopadhyay in his "Introduction" to *Collected Plays in Translation* observes:

> Power and violence as the natural instrumentality that power brings into play provide the general space in which Tendulkar's plays are played out. As a matter of fact, he [Tendulkar] chose the emerging patterns of violence as his theme for a project when he was awarded the Nehru Fellowship. In an interview soon after the completion of the project, he said that for two years he had moved around the country alone trying to look into situation ranging from individual violence to political movement; covering criminality, the functioning of the police force, the judiciary, jails and the political aspect of violence (xii).

At the end of it Tendulkar grew his interest to know more and more about violence. He was left with a

> curiosity about violence—not as something that exists in isolation, but as a part of the human milieu, human behaviour, human mind. It has become an obsession. At a very sensitive level violence can be described as consciously hunting some one, whether it is physical violence or psychological violence. . . . Violence is something which has to be accepted as a fact. It is no use describing it as good or bad. Projection of it can be good or bad.

> Violence when turned into something else can certainly be defined as vitality which can be very useful, very constructive. So it depends on how you utilize it or curb it at times. (Tendulkar 7)

In his major plays Tendulkar undertakes to study power and violence with a clear vision. The playwright institutionally defines these two predominant themes in his plays, such as the power of media in *Kamala*, the power of performance in *Silence! The Court is in Session,* the power of family in *The Vultures,* the power of State in *Ghashiram Kotwal,* the power of society and morality in *Kanyadaan* and the power of sex in *Sakharam Binder.* In this connection Samik Bandyopadhyay aptly observes: "Tendulkar studies power and violence in spaces institutionally defined the specificities move often than not serving to camouflage the violence in the exercise of power. The institutions that are exposed with their power mechanisms include media (*Kamala*), performance (*Silence! The Court is in Session*), the family (*The Vultures*), the State (*Ghashiram Kotwal*) and (*Encounter in Umbugland*), society and morality (*Kanyadaan*) and sexual mores (*Sakharam Binder*) and (*A Friend's Story*). As the institutions come to embody power, power assumes institutional body, its practice defined and determined within the parameters of the particular institution" (xlii). Thus Tendulkar's art lies not only in the themes he chooses but also in the delineation of his characters.

III

On developing his art, Tendulkar says that his writing always begins with a germ or an idea, sometimes just an incident someone has narrated or a person who has met him maybe for a brief time but left him guessing as to what kind of character he or she can be, or even a news item which he read in the morning paper can even be some other play. Thus Tendulkar's art is developed from his constant observation and critical analysis of men and situations he encounters.

Tendulkar presents the theme of power even through woman. According to Samik Bandyopadhyay:

> His exercise generally falls into a pattern that protects a woman as both provocateur and victim and of a somewhat marginalized observer-confidante, who often doubles as narrator-commentator. The body of the woman and the institutional body of power come into collision in Tendulkar's plays, sparking off and calling forth varying intensities of violence. It is this pattern that offers what Foucault would call 'the point of articulation of the ethical preoccupation and of the political struggle for the respect of rights, of the critical reflection against the abusive techniques of the government and of the ethical research which allows individual liberty to be founded (xlii).

Tendulkar's art can be clearly analyzed in terms of his characterization and structure. In Tendulkar's own words, "a playwright must possess two skills. One: the skill of characterization. The other one: the sense of structure. The first one really speaking is a literary skill. We need literary skill when we write fiction. Without characters no fiction exists. But the skill of characterization in fiction is not exactly the same as the skill required in playwriting. In a fiction we narrate a character. We describe it in words at length. It includes even what happens in its mind from time to time" (ii).

In a play which is to be performed, this kind of description will not work. The character must come to life at the most in a minute, after it enters the stage. Its general get up can certainly help as a kind of visual description and can tell something about the character, but after that the character will speak for itself. It means the dialogue. Even in fiction, we have dialogue. Some fiction has more, some less. There are few short stories and novels which have mostly dialogue and hardly any narrative. They are different from plays. Yet we and even the authors call them fiction and not play.

Dialogue plays an important role in a play more than in a fiction because it establishes the character as a living and a real person and not a cardboard character or the mouthpiece of the playwright. The choice of words signifies the culture of the person, his or her region, profession and the whole background. The speech pattern helps the playwright particularize the character and make it an individual rather than type.

Tendulkar's art of characterization is unique as well as different. His characters have always been related to certain living persons quite a few times because of an obvious similarity of a few details. He never had one single living person in his mind as his character. Even if he had at the beginning of the play the character took its own shape as it moved through the play and changed considerably in the course of development of the play. The final product was a combination of many things which could not be related to one single person in real life. But many times different characteristics of different persons, known and unknown, combined automatically to form a character in his play at the very conceptual level. The incident may be factual but the characters do not remain so. They and the incidents turn themselves into fiction. The final test is how close to reality is the fiction in the play.

The character of Ghashiram in his play *Ghashiram Kotwal* is a classic example in support of this contention. Ghashiram is a very important minor character in our history. No authentic and detailed material is available on this character. Besides, the theme Tendulkar had in mind was not historical, but contemporary and universal. The playwright had to bring Ghashiram to life all by himself. Thus, in the play the character of Ghashiram is a combination of various details historical and contemporary. His visual image and his speech come from images of a few folk form that the playwright had casually seen in his part of the country. So his character is a blend of real life Ghashirams of Tendulkar's times. The playwright did not do it methodically at all. Everything came together by itself, most unmathematically came out and sprang to life just like that on the paper and on the stage of his mind. Ghashiram became a living person to the dramatist after that till he completed, writing the play.

Another good example of how a character takes a shape and life in Tendulkar's play is of Sakharam from his play *Sakharam Binder*. The dramatist never met a man like Sakharam. But he was once told about a man who worked as a binder in a printing press in a small town and lived a strange kind of life. He did not marry, but he was on the look out for a woman who was thrown out by her husband whom he brought home and stayed with her till one of the two got fed up of the other. Then he reached her where she wished to go. He gave her a pair of sarees, some money and little things she would need. Then, he would start his search for a fresh destitute married woman anew. It was a contract marriage without the rites. The contract ended by mutual consent. This was all the dramatist was told. It remained somewhere in his mind. It was not possible for him to go and meet the person to know what kind of a person he could be, how he looked and how he spoke. But something in him intrigued the playwright and it caught the playwright's imagination. Occasionally, Tendulkar would narrate what he had heard of the person to his friends. While narrating inadvertently and sometimes knowingly the playwright kept adding imaginary details to the original version.

The dramatist began describing him in more details. Once he said that he had met him and narrated their meeting which was pure fiction. The narrative went on becoming more detailed. While narrating the episode to Dr. Shree Ram Lagoo, the actor-director in Tendulkar's theatre, he suddenly felt that he could make the character breathe, and he was the central character in the play *Sakharam Binder*. When he wrote the play, the other characters came into the play by their own logic. Tendulkar did not know who the second woman would be in his life till Champa entered the play. She had to have a husband and her husband entered after her, looking for her. Champa was not thrown out by her husband like the first woman, Laxmi; she on her own had walked out on him. She was a combination of three different women the dramatist had come across much before that. One of the three was from an autobiography written by an actress. She was in part that actress and much more.

The art of Tendulkar's characterization is a creative process which is a complicated process. Though the character would appear before Tendulkar in a flash, the details from many sources had unintentionally been stored in the mind for years. They remained dormant without getting processed or used with lots of useless information in utter chaos till the moment of conception arrived. This movement could not be ordered to come. It would come by its own logic.

Tendulkar waited for days trying to conceive a set of characters as real life people until he could see them moving, doing things by themselves, until he heard them emoting, talking to one another. He never began writing his play only with an idea or a theme in mind. He had to have his characters first with him, though not all of them, the ones he needed to begin writing the play, living persons leading him into the thick of their lives where they would give him the theme. At least symbolically speaking Tendulkar did not lead his characters, instead they led him. They showed him the way and he followed them on their trial.

Thus the characters, as part of Tendulkar's art, were the product of his mind, the author's mind, the mind of the creator. But they were not the puppets, not the kings and queens on a chess board whom he pushed and moved at his convenience, but living persons of distinction. That is why they were in his play with their own minds, ways and destiny. He took all this into cognizance. He respected all this and wrote his play. In one sense it is their play, not his. It had to be playwright's ultimately because he would have to own it. He confesses honestly that he was never a master of himself while writing his plays. Factors beyond his control and even beyond his knowledge influenced them. He wrote them but he did not know how they got written.

They came to him from somewhere. They pressurized him to write, dogged him, persuaded him, compelled him, made life impossible for him at times and got themselves written. A play basically requires living characters who speak their own language and in their own separate personal style.

Tendulkar's art can be seen in the structural aspect of his plays. By structure Tendulkar does not mean the plot or the story. Structure is not either. It is the total form or the framework of the play. Even a play without a coherent plot or a story must have a structure.

Tendulkar's idea of structure springs from his conviction that in a performing art, the structure is not seen but felt. We can cite number of examples where the performance of a play could not consistently involve the audience and make a sharp impact despite several good points because of a faulty structure. As stated earlier, structure is not the story. Even a good story lacking a good structure has failed. A performing structure is not static. It flows. It has a fluent and steady movement. Its foundation is the undercurrent of the performance. In the case of Tendulkar's art it is the undercurrent or the principle or the theme or the essence or the binding element of the play which makes it one piece and unique and unlike all other plays. It has to be strong and long-lasting if the play has to have durability. Plays with weak structure are seen and even enjoyed in parts for a time, but they slip into oblivion.

Audience is an important factor to judge the art of the playwright. A playwright cannot choose his/her audience. It keeps changing from performance to performance. Each one of them understands and interprets the play in an individual way in the light of his or her experience and understanding of life. The interpretation of nine out of ten cases is different from the playwright's experience and his understanding of life which has led him to write the play. For instance, we can take up Tendulkar's plays, *Sakharam Binder* and *Kanyadaan*. Tendulkar is always aware of his audience, but with a difference. In the case of *Sakharam Binder*, the objections were often raised against some scenes as being violent. Tendulkar was accused of deliberately choosing sensational themes to get cheap publicity; of writing a crude, non-artistic play that destroyed the sanctity of Marathi stage. Tendulkar was shocked by the attacks on him. He said that "every play was not for every body. Those who like what a play has to say, like the play: those who don't like its content don't like it" (Gokhale 31).

IV

If we analyze Tendulkar's vision of life, we can understand his approach to society and all other institutions as an individual and as a writer. As an individual—or rather as a social being—he feels deeply involved in the existing state of his society because he is affected by it though not immediately in some cases or not as much as some others are and in his own way brood over it. Once in a while he even does something to relieve himself of the tensions and the anxiety and agitation produced by this brooding; he participates in a protest meeting or a dharna or a fast or a morcha or a satyagraha. He aligns himself with civil liberty organizations. He does it because he finds that society is full of exploitation perpetuated by individuals and organizations.

But when he looks back at what he has written during his career as a playwright and what he has been doing as a conscious social being, he finds that his writing reflects a mind which is distinctly different from the mind which acts in real life as a socially aware person. As a writer he finds himself persistently inquisitive, non-conformist, ruthlessly cold and brutal as compared to the other committed human beings. The writer in him is more analytical than emotionally committed one way or the other. The writer in him raises inconvenient questions instead of choosing his side and passionately claiming thereafter, that it is always the right one. As a social being, Tendulkar is against all exploitation and he passionately feels that all exploitation must end.

As a writer, Tendulkar feels fascinated by the exploited-exploiter relationship and obsessively delves deep into it instead of taking a position against it. That takes him to a point where he feels that this relationship is eternal, a fact of life however cruel, and will never end. Not that he relishes this thought while it grips him, but he cannot shake it off.

Tendulkar's vision of life can be further understood through his candid portrayal of social realism through women characters in his plays. *Silence! The Court is in Session* is a good example. Performed in 1967, it is the first Tendulkar play to become part of the New Indian Drama phenomenon of the Sixties. It is the first significant modern Indian play in any language to centre on woman as protagonist and victim. It locates its heroine Benare not at an acquiescent receiving end, but at a point of conflict whereas an aggressive transgressor of the sexual mores of her community. She challenges the execution or power in absentia. It is part of Tendulkar's dramatic strategy that Benare's immediate persecutors in the play are as powerless as she. All their exertions to cut Benare down to size show more their striving after power than a real exercise of power.

The way the monologue is framed or presented creates a great deal of dramatic effect. The monologue is central to the play and its efficacy is increased with the music from somewhere in the background, the change of light, and the whole court freezing and the sharp stylistic break in tone are added dimensions to it.

Tendulkar's initiation into his art was by trial and error method without any formal training or anyone explaining to Tendulkar even the basic technique. His capital in this medium was his early grooming, opportunities to make mistakes and correct them, a basic curiosity about people and life around him. He had a skill to internalize details of human behaviour at different levels and in different circumstances and good pickup of mannerism of speech.

Tendulkar's art of theatre has been developed in a different way. He learnt his art of theatre mainly by watching plays, more bad plays than good ones. They provoked him into mentally rewriting them, his way to turn them into good plays. He found it to be an excellent exercise. He also internalized the importance of structure in a play and learnt the skills by watching plays than reading them. His unscientific interest lacking any method in other visual mediums as well and music helped him in learning structure and intrinsic rhythm in all good art.

Tendulkar's vision of life can be made out in his own interviews. In an interview to twin artists Abhijeet and Vaibhav he asks them questions on his own plays like "Why *Baby*?," "Why *Sakharam*?" "Is Life Really So Dark and Cruel?" They tell him that his plays are an extrapolation of reality. Baby accepted suffering dutifully the way dark people accepted slavery and slaughter. Acceptance of torture is a way of living. *Baby* is an extrapolation of reality.

On his vision of life and suffering Tendulkar says that he personally doesn't bother about people who haven't seen life. They close their eyes at the sight of suffering as if it does not exist. The fact is that life is dark and cruel; it is just that we do not care for the truth. We do not want to see it because it might make us uncomfortable. If escapism is our way of living then we will fail to see the truth. Tendulkar has not written about hypothetical pain or created an imaginary world of sorrow. Being from a middle class family, he saw the brutal ways of life by keeping his eyes open. His vision of life came from within him as an outcome of his observation of the world in which he lived. If we want to entertain and make merry, he asks us to go ahead, but he says, that he cannot do it. He has to speak the truth.

On classifying "people, emotions, relationships into right-wrong, good-evil, fair-unfair rather than comfortable-uncomfortable," Tendulkar explains, in detail. We lose the ability to see the complete truth, once we tag things like good-bad, right-wrong. He strongly believes that a criminal is not only a criminal. A murderer can also be a loving father. First of all we must not tag the things. What he says is that our words are inadequate to describe the picture in totality. We should not try to get trapped in the dictionary meanings of words. As for Tendulkar, he simply cares to see and keep his eyes open. What comes out in his art of writing is natural, without the conscious effort of convincing or justifying.

On getting courage to write about writer's own weakness in his works, Tendulkar maintains that keeping distance between our experiences and writings helps a lot. It is not necessary to write exactly at the time when we have just experienced something. If we give time, it will give us clarity to see things better. Once we are at a distance from our experiences, when we see things from outside, we write more honestly. Besides, the pain of writing the truth will always be there. He says: "Yeh tapasya ki taraha hai" (It is like a deep penance). We must learn to bear it.

On the writer's research before writing, Tendulkar says that research is not the right word. He says that he does not deliberately try to find out things before he writes. One does not live to write. We live and writing becomes an offshoot from it. He lives his life keeping his eyes open observing things, and then something comes to him from what he had seen before and he writes it down. He feels something and then he expresses his feelings. It comes from within based on how he has loved.

Regarding the process of creativity, Tendulkar opines that he does not do anything in particular to learn the process of creating. But he admits that there are various processes of creativity. It might work for others, but it does not work for him.

On perception of reality, Tendulkar says that the coexistence of the observer and the happening makes the reality. Reality becomes reality only when it is seen. There is nothing like absolute reality. Our perception of what is happening makes the picture of reality. We should not get frustrated. We must write what we see.

On the question whether a writer should be well read, Tendulkar says that a man who just sits in his room and reads books without looking at the outside world is only half a man. But if we observe and read also, then it helps us in sharpening the tool of language. It gives us ways of expression. We learn how to express and our language improves which makes it easy to write. We need not worry about borrowing part as long as we are honest. Our writing will be influenced by our experiences with other people. We will call it borrowing from them. Reading is just another experience.

With regards to beginning of writing as a creative career, Tendulkar says that he had started writing at an early age. But we need not worry about age. It is never too late. Tendulkar maintains that he has friends who started writing at the age of fifty and they write excellently. But we must keep going and it will come naturally.

In yet another interview to Mukta Rajyadyaksha (web), Tendulkar gives an expression to his thoughts on the director's freedom and stage directions. Tendulkar says that he has rarely interfered in any director's interpretation or way of working. He says that he usually fills in a lot of details because he wants to express whatever is in his mind as he writes. He believes that the director is free to do what he or she wants. It has been the same with his film scripts.

Regarding the controversies generated by plays like *Ghashiram Kotwal* and *Sakharam Binder*, Tendulkar says that he wishes he had been given a chance to explain his stand. What he claims is that his writing has always been honest. He says that he has never tackled something he did not understand. Politics had nothing to do with it. Tendulkar admits that it is true that *Ghashiram* was inspired by the rise of the Shivsena in Maharashtra and the transformation of an artist like Bal Thackeray into a mass leader. But the focus of his exploration there, as in most of his other plays, was on human tendencies, human frailties that change people almost overnight. He says that he has written over thirty plays on various themes. There is a plethora of characters. But people still tend to point to those that generated these unnecessary controversies.

Tendulkar's observations on media are significant as he began his career writing for newspapers, then he went on to theatre, films and television. He believes there is hope for the theatre, especially Marathi parallel theatre, with many young people trying to do something meaningful. He says that television disappoints him. He understands the revenue-driven private channels going in for a certain kind of programming but "What on earth" he asks, "Doordarshan is doing." Comparing BBC with Doordarshan, he says that Doordarshan is in a pitiable state. About newspapers, he observes that for them the reader is just a number that adds on to their circulation.

On the theatre as a collective medium, Tendulkar points out that theatre is different. He says that it is possibly the medium he is most comfortable with. There is, he feels, more respect for a writer's word. It is a medium that is open to change from one performance to the next. Speaking of words, Tendulkar really envies musicians, sometimes, vocalists; they can transcend the word quite easily, get away from its heaviness and achieve the unsaid element in communication.

Thus Tendulkar's vision of life is a vision of keen observation and pragmatic approach. The success of Tendulkar as an artist lies in his ability to portray the social realism as it exists and as he sees it. Hence this study.

V

Critical scholarship on Tendulkar has been vast and varied. Critics have examined Tendulkar as a man and as a dramatist from different perspectives—humanistic, philosophical, psychological and historical. Veena Noble Dass considers him not only an artist but also a thinker: "He has genuinely convinced himself and the theatre world and people in general that he poses the cardinal philosophical problems of mankind through his plays." (90)

It is said that Ibsen and his realistic technique have exercised a profound influence on Tendulkar. Veena Noble Dass observes: "This is partially true. . . . Tendulkar's explorations of the real demonstrate his extraordinary power of probing, analyzing and interpreting the moral and psychological states of his characters" (90)

Amol Palekar, an eminent actor, finds in Tendulkar's plays "a sheer range of work with quality and hard-hitting strength" (5). As Nishikant D. Mirajkar rightly puts it: "Tendulkar symbolizes the new awareness and attempts of Indian dramatists of the last quarter century, to depict the agonies, suffocations and cries of man, focusing particularly on those of middle class. He has been vocalizing different human relations and the tensions implied therein, through his plays, which depict the tragic consequences of confrontation of egos in these relations" (37).

Gowri Ramnarayan, a senior journalist, who has studied Tendulkar closely, observes: "With his exposure to Marathi theatre from childhood, and journalistic background, Vijay Tendulkar turned contemporary socio-political situations into explosive drama" (13). According to some critics, Tendulkar embraced the existentialist strand of modernism. "This has led," says Kalindi Deshpande, "to a basic internal contradiction in the dramatist's vision; his courting of the alienationist philosophy precludes any possibility of amelioration in the lot of the wretched-of-the-earth so brilliantly portrayed by him" (14).

Arundhati Banerjee observes the sociological outlook in his plays. In her "Introduction" she remarks: "In all his early plays, Tendulkar is concerned with the middle class individual set against the backdrop of a hostile society" (vii). Shanta Gokhale examines humanistic approach in his plays: "For Tendulkar the primary compulsion is and has always been humanistic. Man's fight for survival, the varied moralities by which people live, the social position of women, the covert or overt violence in human beings, these are his abiding concerns. They appear in his plays in different forms" (32).

Sudhir Sonalkar, a critic, finds psychological realism in the play *Silence! The Court is in Session*: "It is about the innate savagery in all of us" (20-26). Shubha Tiwari sees the play as a strong social commentary and comments on the gender discrimination of the society reflected in the play: "The behavioural case that society has created for a woman is very congested, tight, suffocating and rigid" (38). Tendulkar believes that violence is not only a basic quality but also innate nature of man. By operating the technique of play-with-in-the-play and using the asides, long monologues and symbols like green cloth parrot and songs, Tendulkar achieved almost 'Pirandellesque' effect (Banerjee 572).

Smita Mishra's perspective of the play *Ghashiram Kotwal* is not only political but also sociological. She examines the play as "the destruction of meaningful human relationships and social and moral values." (68) N.S. Dharan analyzes the play as a universal political reality: "The inescapable reality is that as long as politics remains a power game Phadnavis, Ghashirams, and Lalita Gauris are bound to emerge. Not only in India but the world over, we witness, Ghashiram Kotwals being played on real political theaters. This universal political reality in fact accounts for the abiding popularity of the play." (100) Talking about the play which is presented in a variety folk form, Nadkarni feels, "Which is incomparable in the annals of Marathi theatre" (73-74). As Veena Noble Dass rightly observes: "Tendulkar plays are pointed towards an important human predicament, is itself a tribute to the questioning and probing spirit of Tendulkar" (90).

It is evident from the above survey of criticism that though a number of critics of Tendulkar have discussed varied themes and techniques of the plays, there are only stray references to the author's social realism. There is, however, a need to make a full-length study of Tendulkar's portrayal of social realism. Hence the present study.

The study proceeds from the postulate that in order to reach the core of Tendulkar's themes, his social realism should be fully explored. Among the fifty-four plays Tendulkar wrote including one-act plays, my study is limited to the five of Tendulkar's major plays to bring out the treatment of social realism, namely *Silence! The Court is in Session*, *Sakharam Binder*, *Ghashiram Kotwal*, *Kanyadaan* and *Kamala* which are the finest expression of his social realism. They enrich the tone and tenor of the modern society.

Tendulkar's thematic presentation of issues like violence, power, phallocentrism, caste politics, disintegration of the institutions of family and marriage in the plays chosen for study here reflect his probing insights into social realism. He may not suggest any remedies to these social problems explicitly in his plays; but it is not difficult to perceive his proclivities especially in the light of his radically progressive views.

Works Cited

Bandyopadhyay, Samik. Introduction. *Collected Plays in Translation* by Vijay Tendulkar. Calcutta: Seagull, xlii-lii. 1984.

Banerjee, Arundhati. Introduction. *Five Plays by Vijay Tendulkar*. New Delhi: Oxford UP, 1992.vii-xix.

Dass, Veena Noble. "Towards a New Hindi Drama: The Plays of Mohan Rakesh." *Modern Indian Drama in English Translation,* Hyderabad: 1988.

Dharan, N.S. *The Plays of Vijay Tendulkar*. New Delhi: Creative, 1999.

Gokhale, Shanta. "Tendulkar on his own Terms." *Vijay Tendulkar's Plays*: *An Anthology of Recent Criticism*, ed. V.M. Madge.

Hudson, W.H. *An Introduction to the Study of Literature*. New Delhi: Atlantic, 2008.

_____. *An Outline History of English Literature*. New Delhi: Maple Press, 2009.

Madge, V.M. Introduction to *Vijay Tendulkar's Plays*: *An Anthology of Recent Criticism*. Delhi: Pencraft International. 2009. 11-17.

Mirajkar, Nishikant D. "Two Recent Plays of Vijay Tendulkar." *New Directions in Indian Drama,* ed. Pandey and Barua. Delhi: Prestige, 1994.

Mishra, Smita. "Ghashiram Kotwal as a Political Play." *Contemporary Indian Dramatists*, ed. Shubha Tiwari. New Delhi: Atlantic, 2007.

Pinglay, Prachi. "To Preserve a Theatre Tradition." Interview of Amol Palekar. *The Hindu*, folio on theatre. 30 Oct. 1998.

Shukla, Supriya. "Indian English Drama: An Introduction." *Perspectives and Challenges in Indian English Drama*, ed. Neeru Tandon. New Delhi: Atlantic, 2006.

Singh, Brijraj. "*Sakharam Binder*: A Reappraisal." *New Quest*. 6 Feb. 1978.

Sircar, Badal. *The Third Theatre.* Based on project entitled "Workshop for a Theatre of Synthesis as Rural Urban Link" published by Badal Sircar. Calcutta: 1978.

Sonalkar, Sudhir. "Vijay Tendulkar and the Metaphor of Violence." *The Illustrated Weekly of India.* Nov. 20-26, 1983: 30.

Tendulkar, Vijay. "Afterword," *Kanyadaan.* Delhi: Oxford UP. 1996.

Tendulkar, Vijay. "Introduction," *Ghashiram Kotwal.* Calcutta: Seagull. 1984.

Tendulkar, Vijay. "Natak Ani Mee." Interview. Shirish Pai and Priya Tendulkar. Thane: Dimple, 1997.

Tendulkar, Vijay. "The Play is the Thing," Sri Ram Memorial Lecture. Lecture No. I. New Delhi: Sri Ram Centre for Performing Arts. 1997.

Tiwari, Shubha. "*Silence! The Court is in Session*: A Strong Social Commentary." *Contemporary Indian Dramatists*, ed. Shubha Tiwari. New Delhi: Atlantic, 2007.

Silence! The Court is in Session: A Feminist Attack on Patriarchy

Vijay Tendulkar was the first playwright to take up as his major theme the Indian middle class like Arthur Miller in the 1950s and the 60s. Vijay Tendulkar's words, "As a social being I am against all exploitation and I passionately feel that all exploitation must end" (147), are an evidence that establish him as a dramatist with social consciousness. Tendulkar's every play is a reflection on the existing conditions of the society. If *Ghashiram Kotwal* is a reflection on women's exploitation in power politics, *Kamala* is on sensational journalism and male chauvinism, while *Sakharam Binder* is on diluting human relationships and institution of marriage, *The Vultures* on domestic violence and degeneration of human values and *Kanyadaan* on hypocritical values and caste politics.

The play *Silence! The Court is in Session* is studied and interpreted as a realistic exposure of urban middle class morals and a documentary of gyno-centricism, where premarital sex and abortion are debated from the perspective of women emancipation. It can be seen as a perfect mockery of existing judicial system in India. The play is nothing but a satire which exposes male-biased arrangement of the elite-court relations in India and oppression of women legitimized by legal regulations. As such, the title *Silence! The Court is in Session* is self-explanatory.

Tendulkar's plays are replete with such theatrical craft that a good production is possible by simply following his stage directions. In this context, Vikram Gokhale remarks:

> There is an invisible director in Tendulkar who keeps making a variety of suggestions to the adventurous playwright in him from

> time to time. Once in a while the sensitive spectator and the ruthless critic in him also prick and prod the playwright. That is why the playwright walks along the straight path of truth to the predetermined end, strewing brackets as he proceeds, before, between or after dialogues, filling them with the most valuable stage directions. The guidance they provide to the director, actor and reader is of great help. It is my belief that even a moderately intelligent director or actor would do a good job of Tendulkar play the more gifted of course would reap immense success (95).

Tendulkar got stimulated from a real incident to write the play, *Silence! The Court is in Session.* He met an amateur group which was on its way to stage a mock-trial in Vile Parle, a suburb of Bombay. While overhearing their conversation, the outline of a play began taking shape in the writer's mind and resulted in the creation of *Silence! The Court is in Session* (Tendulkar 15). The play was written for Rangayana at the instance of Arvind and Sulabha Deshpandey and was first performed in March 1971 in Madras.

Tendulkar is unique from other playwrights of contemporary theatre because of his experimentation not only with the subject matter but also with the form and structure of the drama. Though his innovative dramatic techniques and experimental methods in the presentation of varied themes have brought new authenticity and power to the highly orthodox Marathi theatre, his treatment of socially controversial themes and his unconventional approach to human problems in his plays have made him a controversial writer. As a writer of realistic dramas he often electrifies the conservative audiences with brutal themes and direct dialogues. Being a very sensitive writer he observes the social, political, cultural and moral degeneration of contemporary society and presents it in his plays with thorough detachment and clinical objectivity. His usage of techniques like satire, irony, pathos and mock-element effectively criticizes the middle-class mindset and its conventional attitude towards life. Deeply influenced by "real life experiences, hearsay, news items, films, plays and literature in general" (Banerjee x), Tendulkar portrays the physical sufferings and mental agonies which arise out of man's conflict with the hostile surroundings in which he lives. As a social scientist he visualizes human angst and predicament and presents it with a great analysis in his plays. He depicts not only the confrontation between society and individual but also modern man's total failure to understand either himself or others in the society. He would not simplify or generalize man, "the complex phenomenon." Tendulkar himself admits: "It's an obsession with me to capture human behaviour, elusive and ever changing. At every stage, what I perceived has been reflected in my work. It's not that I am writing now on a conclusion reached long ago" (172).

Obviously his approach to life is quite affirmative and his uncompromising commitment to human values is found in all his plays. Among the plays written by Tendulkar the most popular and prominent are *Silence! The Court is in Session, Sakharam Binder*, *Ghashiram Kotwal, Kanyadaan* and *Kamala.*

The play *Silence! The Court is in Session* exposes the gender bias which is rooted in patriarchal system of Indian society. The play is nothing but a feministic attack on Indian society. Tendulkar perceives the realities of the human society without any pre-occupied notions, reacts to them as a sensitive and sensible human being and writes about them in his plays as a responsible writer. The play indirectly exposes the cruel nature inherent in our so called 'elite' and 'judicial' male-dominated society. Tendulkar was inspired by a case in which an unwed mother was sentenced to life for committing the same crime that is done by the protagonist in the play. The play is about the pathetic position of women in the 'male dominated' Indian society. Tendulkar's portrayal of the plight, the ponderings, predicaments and problems of a middle class Indian woman is heart-rending. How the very system of justice is also gender-biased is powerfully exposed by him in the present play.

In *Silence! The Court is in Session*, Leela Benare is young, single, unconventional, full of laughter and pride. On the other hand, she ignores social norms and dictates. She yearns for equality with men in their own world. In her view, men must prove themselves before they can command her respect. She has an illicit love affair with a married man and gets pregnant but he does not have the guts to own his child. At last she becomes a prey to the hypocrisy and double standards of the male chauvinistic society.

The marvellous use of the technique 'the play within the play' gives the whole play a new dimension. It indirectly exposes the cruel nature inherent in our so-called 'elite' and 'judicial' male-dominated society. The intellectual who is responsible for Benare's humiliating condition goes unscathed and unnoticed, but she is dragged literally naked in front of those men. The very men who give lectures on the dignity of women and motherhood are responsible for inflicting shame and indignity on her. Slow but steady development of so-called illusive 'mock-trial' into a serious affair with the sudden charges and stunning blames in an extraordinary sombre and tense atmosphere resembles our modern courts.

In fact, the play and its structure revolve wholly round the idea of a game and include the essential ingredient of 'reversal' of the 'natural justice.' The dialogues in the play are characterized by a certain idiosyncratic use of syntax. Most of the utterances are short and there are abundant pauses, marked by numerous dots and dashes. Without taking much pain, the 'demotic' and 'rounded' style of dialogues can convince the audience about the 'bare faced lies' of the characters.

The play can be interpreted as a 'legal plea' which demands emancipation, equality and liberation of women and emphasizes the need for a social transformation of law, culture, and social patterns which release women's potential, where the legal curriculum has neglected issues of central concern of women like rape, domestic violence, reproduction, unequal pay, sex determination and sexual harassment. Indian constitution ensures women 'equality before the law' prohibits 'any discrimination' and guarantees 'equality of opportunity for all citizens.' Though, various enactments have tried to bring certain degree of emancipation of Indian women in a legal sense, the legal position, however, is far from being satisfactory. Women are not enjoying these rights and suffer from a number of socially inexorable disabilities and inhibitions. The position of women in middle-class families is even worse. They usually do not exercise their rights owing chiefly to the constraints of the existing society, therefore, are unable to achieve the legal equality with men. The social structure, norms and values in the patriarchy, which govern human behaviour do not favour women using their rights and thus create obstacles towards the enforcement of legislations.

As an artist and explorer of personal life, Tendulkar not only unmasks these realities but also expounds the mental sufferings of their victims. When asked in an interview: "This play is a caustic satire on the social as well as legal justice . . . the mental agony suffered by the girl throughout the play is in no way less than the legal punishment. Is that all you wished to convey or something more?" Tendulkar said:

> This is exactly what I had in mind. If I say anything else now, that will be an after-thought. An undaunted girl of Benare's make-up could have, besides defending herself, made a counter attack, tearing to pieces the dos and don'ts of the selfish society. Had I shown her aggressive that would have been attitude, not hers? Otherwise also the playwright should only suggest leaving the rest to the viewers. (280)

Though the social issues discussed in *Silence! The Court is in Session* are not quite organically integrated into its plot, the plot is expertly structured so that the denouement unravels itself as 'reversal.' Its 'setting' is the city and the 'atmosphere' is tense throughout with only occasional patches of 'comic relief.'

It is the imposed silence of Benare that gives the title its unique significance. Till the 'commencement of the mock-trial,' Benare remains a picture of poise and vitality. She makes comments on the behaviour of her fellow-characters and sits singing and humming. Nevertheless silence descends on her when the 'mock-trial' begins with Kashikar's sudden interrogative statement: "Prisoner Ms. Benare, under section No. 302 of the Indian Penal Code you are accused of the crime of infanticide. Are you guilty or not guilty of the aforementioned crime?" (74)

Benare is dumbfounded. Even the comic relief provided by the pan-spitting contest helps her regain her composure only for a brief while. As the mock-trial is resumed, Benare increasingly seeks shelter in her self-imposed silence. Further, all her attempts to protest are drowned in Kashikar, the mock judge's imposition: "Silence!" In such a helpless, hostile situation, Benare has no other choice but to remain silent, as no language can come to her rescue.

However, Benare breaks her forced silence at last, towards the end of the play, when she bursts out into a long and brilliant monologue which brings out in most eloquent terms, her love-life, focusing with astonishing brilliance on her betrayal at the hands of Prof. Damle, and the consequent torture at the hands of her fellow-characters. In fact, it is this monologue that has captured the imagination of the audience of the Marathi theatre. Tendulkar deliberately makes Benare break her silence through this stunning monologue which exposes the hypocrisy of the urban middle class male chauvinists who have all ganged up against her out of sheer collective envy of her assertive confidence and uncompromising independence of spirit.

In fact Tendulkar's use of monologues in his plays is not new to the Marathi audience. His dealing with the themes like love, sex, marriage, violence, gender inequality, social inequality, power games, alienation and individual isolation force Tendulkar to use self-justifying speeches sometimes in the form of a soliloquy that give vent to some suppressed sorrow and for explaining the person's behaviour. These kinds of monologues are delivered by Rama, Benare, Ghashiram and

Arun. The monologues in *Ghashiram Kotwal* are significantly lengthy. In *Sakharam Binder* Sakharam introduces himself in a lengthy speech. When Tendulkar was asked why he had used such lengthy monologues, he replied: "Soliloquy is not very meaningful by itself. It does not interest me as a form. It has been used because the theme demanded it." (Dass 202)

The 'mock trial' marks a deft-stroke on the part of Tendulkar. It functions almost like a 'play-within-the-play,' as the real performance is supposed to have been 'Mock Law Court.' It is the 'mock-trial' that causes the terminal 'reversal' in the play. Benare, who has earlier been sprightly, ends up being the game ruthlessly hunted and baited by her male counterparts. This element of 'reversal' gives the play its unique dramatic significance. The 'mock trial' also helps the playwright expose to his audience the cruelty that is latent in the collective psyche of the city-bred men and the naked display of their innate cruelty towards her. The eagerness and enthusiasm with which the Kashikars, Rokde, Sukhatme, Ponkshe and Karnik heap evidence after evidence against her terrify her and eventually, she sits frozen like a motionless statue.

Structurally, the songs Tendulkar assigns to Benare are of great dramatic significance. For instance take the song sung by Benare in the opening scene.

> Oh I've got a sweetheart
> Who carries all my books,
> He plays in my doll house,
> And says he likes my books.
> I'll tell you a secret—
> He wants to marry me.
> But mummy says, I'm too little
> To have such thoughts as these. (58-59)

The song carries dramatic significance, as it anticipates Karnik's disclosure of Benare's fruitless love for her maternal uncle in the third Act. The second song, a nursery-rhyme, also appears in the very same scene:

The grass is green
The rose is red
The book is mine
Till I am dead. (62)

The lines are again significant in that Benare realizes, in the course of the play, that she has nothing that she can call her own. More important than these two compositions in verse is the one which she recites it in the opening scene:

Our feet tread upon unknown
And dangerous pathways evermore. . . .
And the wound that's born to bleed
Bleeds on forever, faithfully.
There is a battle sometimes, where
Defeat is destined as the end.
Some experiences are meant
To taste, then just to waste and spend. (63)

It is from the above Marathi poem by Mrs. Shirish Pai that Tendulkar has conceived Benare, the central character in the play. In accordance with the above aphoristic kind of verse, Benare feels that she is destined to be defeated in the end. Another ballad-like verse favoured by Benare is:

The parrot to the sparrow said,
'Why, oh why are your eyes so red?'
'Oh, my dear friend, what shall I say?
Someone has stolen my nest away.'
Sparrow, sparrow, poor little sparrow! (74)

Benare sings it to herself towards the end of Act I and repeats it again at the end of Act III where it supposedly emerges from an indistinct source in Benare's voice. The 'parrot' in the play is suggestive of Samant and the 'nest' may refer to her chastity which she is deprived of by Professor Damle and 'the crow' too seems to be none other than the hard-hearted and selfish Professor himself.

The playwright introduces the paan-spitting context as a comic interlude in order to relieve the gloom of the immediately preceding sombre atmosphere. At the time of serious issues, the dialogues pick up a faster rhythm and the sentences, a certain depth and fullness. Rokde's witness is laced with 'demotic style.' Style easily makes audience realize how Rokde says a bare-faced lie and how today's courts are a replica for exercising gimmicks of the tongue twists. This is realism that Tendulkar exposes in the play. "So then—so then I said—this isn't proper. It's not proper—I—I—don't like this at all—It doesn't become you—that's what I said." (102)

The play is free from any easily recognizable flaws. The playwright does not indulge even for a moment in any of this for the sake of sheer theatricality. The situations evolve and unfold themselves rather gradually. The 'reversals' surprise not only the characters in the play but the readers and spectators as well. The audiences have the satisfaction of having witnessed a few rarified moments of pure aesthetic delight and intellectual insight designed by an utmost powerful artist. The play shows how a woman is tormented in a male-dominated society and how words are more powerful than weapons. The deeper interpretations are to expose the way how inferior, mediocre persons—small men as Shakespeare calls them—trap superior individuals and fulfill their innate burning itch of publicly denouncing them—a kind of character assassination. Because they do not do it openly, they take a chance to achieve their ends by using deceptive ways through mock-trial.

Contextually, it is interesting to know that Tendulkar, like his woman protagonist Benare, was also attacked by many critics for his bare portrayal of the men and morals as he is fond of portraying realism. The treatment of the theme, characterization and the structure of the play reveal his artistic excellence. The play is widely appreciated for its technical experiments, textual compactness, sharp dialogue, skillful art of characterization and brilliant plot construction. The use of irony and satire and the symbols such as the green cloth parrot and the locked door certainly enhance the dramatic effect. Moreover, the excellent combinations in the dramatic narrative of the tragic and comic episodes such as using the English dictionary for a holy book in the process of taking oath, spitting contest and ear-picking during the court proceedings show the real artistry and creative skill of the playwright.

When the play was first performed in 1967 for a drama competition by a small group, it was rejected by the judges. At the time of the staging the play there were so many controversies over its indebtedness to Tennessee Williams' *Different Places* as Tendulkar's own comments on the derivativeness in the preface of the play were not satisfactory. Despite such controversies Tendulkar received The Kamaladevi Chattopadhyaya award for the play and it was translated into fourteen languages. The play was staged all over India in different versions. In other words, Marathi drama found a place on the national map and Tendulkar was recognized at the national level.

Unhesitatingly, the play *Silence! The Court is in Session* not only has brought laurels to Tendulkar as a powerful playwright but also kept his name on the top of Indian modern theatre.

II

The play *Silence! The Court is in Session* has three acts designed in the mode of the popular dramatic construct of the present century. There are no scene divisions of the acts. As the curtain raises, Samant, a local chap and Leela Benare, the protagonist of the play are found conversing. Benare feels light-hearted and happy in Samant's company. Then she talks to Samant of her career as a teacher, saying her pupils are "so much better than adults" (56). When she says these words, she has Professor Damle in her mind—and the audiences realize this fact in the course of the play, especially, when she says: "At least they don't have the blind pride of thinking they know everything. There's no nonsense stuffed in their heads. They don't scratch you till you bleed, then run away like cowards." (57)

Benare, after telling Samant that the school management is holding an enquiry against her "just because of one bit of slander," (58) ignoring the fact that she is in the presence of a stranger, who is in no way connected with her present plight, bursts out, placing her hand on swelling stomach. In her present mental state, it seems, after seeing child-like, plain-spoken Samant, Benare does not feel that he is a stranger. Benare must have seen a 'friend,' a 'confidante' in innocent and rustic Samant to share personal matters of her life.

Gradually Benare regains her poise and sings an English song to herself to show that there was nothing wrong with her. Tendulkar turns the opening scene of the play into a marvellous piece of satire by pitting the self-consciously independent, vehemently assertive and immensely cheerful Benare against the utterly selfish, hypocritical and malicious amateur artists and paves the way as to how they are going to judge and reverse the natural justice. The opening scene also depicts how an average middle class woman strives and struggles for preserving her womanhood and motherhood and her thirst to be accepted by the society.

Benare is presented as the central character in *Silence! The Court is in Session.* It is mainly through her ironic perception that the audience gets an insight into the other characters. She is a responsible school teacher who is as sprightly, rebellious and assertive as the heroines of Shakespeare's romantic comedies, as some critics have already observed. She is conscientious in her work and commands the love and respect of all her pupils. She is also an enlightened activist, being a member of the amateur theatre group called "The Sonar Mati Tenement Progressive Association." (Bombay)

Benare's exploitation begins with her uncle who had exploited her sexually in her teenage. He did not think of marrying her. On the other hand, even her own mother fails to understand or support her. But Benare shows guts. She starts her life all over again, continues her studies and finally settles into a teaching job. As a teacher, she comes in contact with Professor Damle whom she considers quite intelligent, and academically bright. Though married, the Professor exploits her sexually and refuses to marry her. As she is pregnant with the Professor's child, she is desperate to find a way to escape social stigma and humiliation. She requests two of her colleagues at the drama company to marry her. But obviously enough they also refuse to attach their names to her. Her bitter experiences of life made her attack male chauvinism and false concepts of masculinity. Unable to digest this, the actors plan to expose and humiliate her through a mock-trial. She gets into the trap. Once the trial begins, there is no escape for poor Benare.

She is labelled by all dirty adjectives. Professor Damle has been spared the iron rod. It is Benare who is accused of immorality, sin, promiscuity and over-sexuality. The verdict dismisses her from her school job, orders for abortion, and blackens Benare's name forever. Benare reminds us of Kunti, a character in the epic *The Mahabharata*, who becomes pregnant by God Surya out of wedlock. After delivering the child she abandons the infant in a river and later marries Prince Pandu of Hastinapur. Though she is pious and shows fidelity towards her husband, she repents for her coward act later. Whereas Leela Benare is an antithesis of Kunti who shows guts of revealing the fact of her mothering a child when she proposes to two of her colleagues. Here, Benare asserts her individuality, right of choice, right over her own body, right as a human being. She is very much conscious of her identity as a woman and of her civil rights. She asserts: "My life is my own. I haven't sold it off to any one for a job. My mind is my own. My desire is similarly my own. No one can suppress it. No one can decide what to do with it!" (58)

Biological phenomenon is deliberately glorified by the society in order to obtain control over women's sexuality. Societies overlook the sexual offences of men and consider they are not offences at all. Though the sin is committed by both, only women are accused. Society is at its best, most natural and relaxed ground censoring 'bad' women as though there exist 'bad' women without 'bad' men. The whole responsibility of morally upright behaviour is bulldozed on women. Men are by nature, considered to be wilful, wild, childish, innocent and mischievous. Their sins are no sins at all. The society has a very light, parental, and pampering sort of attitude when it comes to sexual offences of men. In case of women the iron rod gets hot and hotter. No punishment is actually enough for such a woman. As Shubha Tiwari points out, "There is no respite, no shade, and no soothing cushion for a sinning woman. She must be stained and abandoned. Her femininity, her needs, her very existence must be ignored, or rather destroyed" (35). She must be cornered and brutally killed—both in physical and psychological senses. The same perspective is shown by Tendulkar in this play. But one thing that is assured in Tendulkar's plays is, that his women seem to be agents of change.

Leela Benare is lively, plain-hearted, outspoken, open-minded, honest and independent in thinking. She is a good and committed teacher who is adored by her students. In her conversation with Samant in the opening scene she remarks:

> I'm used to standing while teaching. In class, I never sit when teaching. That's how I keep my eyes on the whole class. No one has a chance to play up. My class is scared stiff of me! And they adore me, too. My children will do anything for me. For I'd give the last drop of my blood to teach them (58).

Benare is extremely critical about others. She, now, begins to provide Samant with additional information about her co-actors. It is mainly through her ironic perception that the audiences get an insight into the other characters. She sarcastically refers to Mr. Kashikar as "Mr. Prime Objective" (59) and Mrs. Kashikar as "Mrs. Hand-that-Rocks-the-Cradle" (59). She says: "Mr. Prime Objective is tied up with uplifting the masses. And poor Hand-that-Rocks-the-Cradle has no cradle to rock" (59). Benare also informs Samant that childless Kashikars have adopted Balu

Rokde in order to escape their boredom in life and in the process have made a slave of the poor fellow:

> Mr. Kashikar and the Hand-that-Rocks-the-Cradle, in order that nothing should happen to either of them in their bare, bare house and that they shouldn't die of boredom!—gave shelter to a young boy. They educated him. . . . Made a slave out of him (59).

Benare's description of her colleagues is marked with a bitter sarcasm. She refers to Sukhatme as "an Expert on the law" (59). Ironically, "he's such an authority on the subject, even a desperate client won't go anywhere near him! He just sits alone in the barrister's room at court, swatting flies with legal precedents! (59). Ponkshe, to her, is a 'Hmm! Sci-en-tist! Inter failed!" (59). Benare then foretells that Professor Damle, though one of the actors in the troupe, will not dare to come:

> And we have an intellectual too. That means someone who prides himself on his book learning but when there's a real-life problem, away he runs! Hides his head. He's not here today. Won't be coming, either. He wouldn't dare! (60)

It is for Samant's benefit only that they discuss the feasibility of holding a mock-trial. Sukhatme entertains his audience by telling them of various games lawyers play in the barrister's room, when they have leisure in the court. One such game is to bring an imaginary case against someone and hold a mock-trial. The words 'imaginary case' and 'mock-trial' suggest the reliability of judicial circle.

As Miss Benare too likes the idea and finds it funny as the hopscotch she plays with children at school, all agree to send Samant away to fetch some cigarettes and pan. Benare retires to the wash room to get refreshed. During her short absence, Ponkshe, Karnik, Sukhatme and Mrs. Kashikar discuss the question of cast and decide who should be the accused. According to their pre-planned conspiracy, they unanimously agree that the accused will be Benare. All set, as soon as Ms. Benare returns humming a song to herself, Kashikar in his thunderous, magisterial voice charges her: "(clearing his throat) Prisoner Miss Benare, under the section No. 302 of the Indian penal code you are accused of the crime of infanticide. Are you guilty or not guilty of the aforementioned crime?" (75). Benare says: "I couldn't kill even a common cockroach. I am scared to do it. How could I kill a newborn child?" (79). The men in the court paid deaf ear to the words of Benare. Benare's innocence was not considered and they all seem to have ganged up against her. Benare herself observes their odious nature by saying, "You have all deliberately ganged up against me! You have plotted against me" (93).

Thus, the "game" begins as the stage direction says at the end of the first act, in the atmosphere which is "extraordinarily sombre." All these suggest how only women, especially charged with illegal conduct, suffer between gossip-mongering public associates of day-to-day life as well as legal inquisitions.

Even before Ms. Benare can answer her charge, Samant returns with the packet of cigarettes and paan followed by a paan-chewing and spitting contest. The proceedings begin with Sukhatme as the prosecution lawyer, with his mouth full of pan pleading for an adjournment of fifteen seconds to enable him spit out the juice, and again, changing into the role of defence counsel raises objections to the length of the adjournment and reduces it to ten seconds. Even Ms. Benare, the accused, forgetting the court procedure joins in the fun and reduces it still further to 9.5 seconds. Kashikar, the judge, wants to know if there is any legal precedent for such an adjournment and is informed that it is not there. Half a minute is thus wasted to decide on the fifteen-second adjournment. But when Ms. Benare proposes to change the charge from infanticide to robbery of public property, the scandal-loving audience wants to retain the original accusation. Once again there is a difference between men and women in the sight of law and justifies Samant's question: "Does a real-court truly work like this?" (77)

However, Tendulkar chooses different persons from different backgrounds perhaps to give the audience some clues about the judicial circle and their judicial culture. He wants to show the real scenario of the present-day courts and their loopholes. In fact, all these characters are the representatives of the existing personalities in judicial circles with all defects. Mr. Kashikar's prime objective is to uplift the masses where he utterly fails in his personal as well as familial life. Mr. Kashikar's relation with Mrs. Kashikar in the play brings out the humiliation and subjugation of the typical Hindu Brahmin wife in an orthodox family. The very fact of Mrs. Kashikar's collusion in the attack on Benare demonstrates how women internalize the dominance of men over themselves as a natural phenomenon. The power of family as an ideological state apparatus lies in its function of reproducing conditions in which women learn to submit to the rules of established patriarchal order. Mrs. Kashikar is a case in the play.

Mrs. Kashikar is conventional and does not have good opinion of 'independent' women like Benare. She is also a social worker who has her role in the prime objective of uplifting masses who are depressed and suppressed. The most important thing in the play about her is that she is childless. As a woman she can understand the pain of barrenness as well as pre-marital pregnancy. But, she, in no way is less than those men, in cruelly drawing blood when Benare is put on trial. Mrs. Kashikar could not have ever admitted even to herself that it is on account of the sacrosanct institution of marriage that she is open to Mr. Kashikar's constant insults and snubs. He feels he has an automatic right to do so by virtue of being a man and her husband. Despite the insults, she considers him as a caring husband, as much by her as by others, because he has bought a string of flowers for her hair, a token not of just love, but romance. When she is asked why Miss Benare had remained single till such an 'advanced' age, her response is:

> That's what happens these days when you get everything without marrying. They just want comfort. They couldn't care less about responsibility! Let me tell you my time, even if a girl was snub-nosed, sallow, hunchbacked, or anything whatever, she-could-get-married! It's the sly fashion of women that makes everything go wrong. That's how promiscuity has spread throughout our society. (99-100)

It is obvious that the working educated women have higher concern for status than the non-working women or housewives. Concern for status among educated women has deeper roots in personality and is closely related to certain personality dispositions. It has been found positively not only related to ego-strength and emotional stability but also to economic independence. Concern for status bears significant relationship with value orientations like liberalism, non-authoritarianism, and scientism. All the relationships of these values are influenced by interactional affects of age, employment and some other social, personal background factors. However, the way things are, there is no choice for Mrs. Kashikar but to be a participant in the patriarchal system.

Mrs. Kashikar is a replica of few women in our society who are denied freedom of speech by their husbands. Being psychologically suppressed by their husbands all the time, ironically these women show hypocritic fidelity towards their husbands. Out of the sweltering state of their disgust, disappointment, demotivation, and dissatisfaction these women show disintegration with their fellow women by joining hands with their men. This is another dimension we see in Tendulkar's portrayal of his women characters.

Sukhatme, Balu Rokde, Gopal Ponkshe and Karnik are the various typical personalities in judicial circle. The commencement of the "mock-trial" which constitutes a 'play-within-the-play' offers Tendulkar enough scope to dissect and lay bare the dormant ills of discontent in the psyche of these urban hypocrites. Though they gang themselves up against a hapless Benare for the time being, they have nothing but spite for one another.

Sukhatme, whom Benare considers as an 'Expert on the Law,' 'an authority on the subject' and 'a great barrister' and 'even a desperate client won't go anywhere near him!,' poses himself that he has instant solutions for the great problems of the law. With respect to the problem caused by Rawat's absence, Sukhatme suggests Samant as Rawat's substitute. When Mrs. Kashikar suggests a rehearsal with Samant, Sukhatme agrees with her and suggests "a new and imaginary case against someone" (71) so that Samant may understand how the court functions. He is quick to add, before Benare, "this is just a game" (71). He is the only person who constantly reminds both Benare and Samant that what happens around them is only 'a game' and allows others to torture Benare ruthlessly. Sukhatme enquires of Benare: "Why are you so grave all of a sudden? After all, it's a game. Just a game, that's all. Why are you serious?" (75) The deceiving nature of Sukhatme knows no bounds when he says to Samant: "for the sake of the trial we're taking something for granted" (90) and convinces an innocent witness. All his questions as the lawyer for prosecution are not legally persuasive but emotionally targeted towards Benare. He always puts the client on stand and barbs with ruthless logic by asking questions like: "Miss Benare, the game's really warmed up! Hasn't it?" (101) and walking around in front of Benare for a while suddenly points a finger at her and says: "your name is Leela Damle." All these things show that Mr. Sukhatme's role in the play is a replica of the legal professionalism and an evidence of how "there is a fall in efficiency and standard at the Bar and which is on the verge of collapse." The legal profession is no longer service-oriented but profit-oriented. Sometimes lawyers on both sides join hands to make both the parties compromise even if the clients have to suffer the laws. Majority of the lawyers harass their clients for more and more fee, false bills, while not taking the required interest in the case.

When Sukhatme begins the prosecution's argument on motherhood, Miss Benare asks him how he, being a man knows about motherhood to be a sacred thing! It gives a picture of the same inherent and latent limitations of the law. There are some aspects that men cannot understand regarding women. A judge or a lawyer may be an expert in law but they are poor in studying the sensitive areas of human personality with a human touch.

Rokde's abject dependence on the arrogant Kashikars, his parasitic life forces him to obey his patrons by providing a false witness against Benare. He obediently goes and stands in the witness-box after Kashikar gives him protection: "Afraid? Why should he be? There's some law and order here, isn't there? (102). Throughout the play, Rokde is not allowed enough time to exercise his intelligent challenges to the judges.

Ponkshe and Karnik are the other two persons who have their active role in the plot against Benare. When Benare goes into the inner room to wash her face, Karnik takes Ponkshe aside and indicating the inner room into which Benare has just gone, tells him if he knows anything about her: "About her, about Miss Benare. Rokde told me" (72). Ponkshe, too, says: "I've got something to tell you, too. About Miss Benare." (72) This aside between Karnik and Ponkshe has a great dramatic significance, as the audiences are to learn soon. It is at Sukhatme's suggestion they all decide to make Benare 'the accused' in the 'mock-trial.' Ponkshe is the first person who accuses Benare: "Miss Leela Benare, you have been arrested on suspicion of a crime of an extremely grave nature and brought as a prisoner before the bar of this court" (74).

Ponkshe provides information about Benare's moral conduct and private life as if he is a great observer of the society but who is an Inter failed scientist. He admits that Benare is a woman who "runs after men too much" (81). Sukhatme, the counsel for the prosecution, calls Ponkshe as his first witness in a tone filled with sarcasm: "My first witness is the world famous scientist, Mr. Gopal Ponkshe. Well, Ponkshe? Are you happy? I've suddenly promoted you to world fame, eh?" (80). Ponkshe has to take his oath, not on *the Gita*, as the custom is but on the Oxford English Dictionary, for Mr. Rokde, the drudge has picked up the fattest book from Mr. Kashikar's house that came to his hand. The irony is he is proud of his acting. For him thinking is feeling. He is such a perfectionist who recommends a dictionary to know the meaning of the words like 'think and feel' and gives definition for 'truth' and 'fiction.'

The next witness called by the judge is Rokde. Rokde the wretch, starts giving his evidence. And from then on, levity gives place to seriousness. It is from this point that the real intention behind the mock-trial becomes clear. Now Miss Benare has no escape from the conspiracy hatched by the men in the name of mock-trial. She is trapped as an innocent deer, in the hands of the cruel hunters. From now on, all of them—Sukhatme, Ponkshe, Karnik, Mrs. Kashikar and even the wretched Rokde—haunt her mercilessly, like vultures. Every detail of her personal life is dragged out into the open and condemned—her 'affair' with Professor Damle, their love, her 'arrogant' behaviour at school with her colleagues and pupils. Nothing is left. She is labelled with all dirty adjectives. When she tries to run away from all this, Mrs. Kashikar goes her way and brings her back to the scene of her torture. Karnik tells the court that it was not Balu who slapped Benare but Benare who slapped Balu. He also tells that Benare did propose to Balu Rokde. Another piece of key information that he tells Kashikar, the mock-judge, is Benare's unsuccessful attempt at suicide when she failed to marry her own maternal uncle with whom she was in love.

Samant, the innocent villager, an outsider to the rest of the group becomes another powerful vehicle of satire against the hypocritical ideal-men, through his utterances and actions. Tendulkar introduces Samant in the play not only to play a vital role in the 'mock-trial' but also to highlight the inhuman and hypocritical nature of his urban counterparts. On being asked by Sukhatme to tell before the 'mock-court' what he saw in

Professor Damle's hostel room, he replies with utmost caution, sensing the sadistic motives of Benare's tormentors, still retaining a bundle of rustic innocence and ignorance. Tendulkar has painted him as only an 'insider' who empathizes with the accused.

Benare, in her monologue, accuses all men as 'hypocrites' whose only interest is in her body and not in her bleeding heart or agonized mind. Commenting on her co-actors, she observes: "These are the mortal remains of some cultural men of the twentieth century. See their faces how ferocious they look! Their lips are full of lovely worn-out phrases! And their bellies are full of unsatisfied desires" (117). How true these comments are for contemporary men! However, the judgments, the hypocrisy of the judges, false witnesses, and the pettiness born out of double standards—all these are valid themes in this play. All the forms of oppression stem from male dominance only. Women are supposed to bear male oppression silently.

The play is, thus, a satire on the conventions and hypocrisy of male-dominated society which is concerned only with a farcical moral code. Talking about social suppression and violence, Millett maintains that "patriarchy is sustained by both ideological and structural factors." The ideological support stems from a system of socialization which conditions both man and woman to accept male domination as 'natural.' Women are socialized into adopting submissive and passive roles and accepting their essentially subordinate position. She identifies the family, the class and the economic and educational systems as the main structural parapets of patriarchy. This is more so in Indian society with a high level of illiteracy and strong traditions of gender inequalities. That is what happens in Benare's case. Certainly, the play *Silence! The Court is in Session* is a case against existing legal curriculum which is fixed in the matrix of patriarchy.

The game of mock-trial which started for entertainment turns into Benare's tragedy. Benare is cross-examined in the court with full mockery. All the other characters like witnesses Mr. Gopal Ponkshe, Mr. Karnik, Rokde, Samant, Counsel for the defence and counsel for the crown Mr. Sukhatme and Judge, Mr. Kashikar and his wife Mrs. Kashikar all behave in a way of mockery. Benare is summoned merely as a witness while she remains the prime accused as the mother of an illegitimate child and having illicit relations with so many persons.

In the beginning of the play, we find Benare bubbling with over-confidence. She represents the working class women who want to be self-reliant and individualistic. The mock-trial holds a mirror to our social response to moral values. Sex is a private affair in one's life. But there are certain social and moral values attached to it. Pre-marital or post-marital sexual relations are condemned in Indian society.

It is most striking to note Benare's defiance of the traditional taboos and demands of marriage with her uncle in a play produced as early as 1967. When society was far more conservative and tradition-bound it was certainly radical of its time. Tendulkar depicts women as being equal underneath their socio-economic class. Silence is a symbol of oppression, a characteristic of the subaltern condition, while speech signifies self-expression and liberation.

Tendulkar is a man of radical and progressive views. His progressive ideology must have made him write with a perspective of women. He has powerfully articulated the socio-political conditions of the contemporary society in his plays. In his words only:

> As an individual or rather as a social being, I feel deeply involved in the existing state of my society (because I am affected by though not immediately in some cases or not as much as some other are) and in my way brood over it once in a way. I even do something to relieve myself of the tension nicely and agitation produced by this brooding. I participated in a protest meeting or dharna or a fast or morcha or a satyagrah. I align myself with some civil liberty organization. As a writer, I find myself persistently inquisitive,

> non-conformist, ruthless, cold and brutal as compared with other committed and human (Tendulkar 147).

Women are exploited by the men and society at large. They suffer in silence. Tendulkar gives the protagonist Benare a different aspect as she voices the injustice made to her and questions the male dominance. Women in literature have been portrayed through centuries as the mythic models from the *Ramayana,* the *Mahabharata* and the *Puranas*. Seeta, Draupadi, Kunti—all were silent sufferers in the matrix of patriarchy whether it was monogamy, polygamy or giving birth to a child out of wedlock.

Benare represents all the women in India who are marginalized, suppressed and oppressed. The judiciary is considered to be one of the four main pillars of democracy. Tendulkar chooses a term of judicial register as the title of his play to show how powerfully patriarchal bias is rooted in our society which denies justice to women. Here, Tendulkar focuses on the maleness of legal proceedings, specifically the trial of sexual crimes like abortion and pre- and extra-marital relationships. Simply, in trials the procedure is designed to break down the story of the woman complainant both by subjecting it to vigorous doubt and by implicitly sexualizing it. The victim becomes an object of the male gaze and forced to relieve her ordeal, which itself becomes another assault.

The violence of the play is fantastically sugar-coated with the technique of the play-within-the-play. Without this technique Tendulkar could not have made his characters directly attack Benare on the charge of infanticide. The play is widely acclaimed for this technique. Dnyaneshwar Nadkarni pays a tribute to the play; "*Silence! The Court is in Session* comes as a turning point in Tendulkar's career. It has a play in rehearsal and a real-life story, and the two intertwine to produce some unusual dramatic confrontations" (Sonalkar 20).

Benare is dismissed from the job. She cries in pain but she does not succumb to the social torture and stands defiant till the end. Reminiscing what she did in the school as a teacher she narrates that she taught the children beauty and purity: "I cried inside, and I made them laugh. I was cracking up with despair, and I taught them hope" (73). As a typical modern and emancipated woman Benare questions the validity of dismissing her from her job. She asks: "For what sin are they robbing me of my job, my only comfort? My private life is my own business. I'll decide what to do with myself; everyone should be able to!" (73). She considers men to be hypocrites whose interest lies only in the body of a woman and not in her sufferings. The cynical game is well-rooted in the sick psyche of the judges that informs the verdict they pass on her, with the sort of sadistic pleasure. The judgement is that her baby should be killed because its existence negates the very idea of moral values.

Mr. Kashikar, the mock judge pronounces the final verdict: "Prisoner Miss Benare, pay the closest attention. Marriage is the very foundation of our society's stability. Motherhood must be sacred and pure. The morality that which you have shown through your conduct was the morality you were planning to impart to the youth of tomorrow. No memento of your sin should remain for future generations. Therefore this court hereby sentences that you shall leave but the child in your womb shall be destroyed" (118-19).

On hearing the inhuman, heartless, merciless and cold-blooded verdict of the judge, Benare writhes in unbearable pain and screams: "No! No! No!—I won't let you do it—I won't let it happen—I won't let it happen!" (76). Terribly upset with the "paroxysms of torment" (76), Benare collapses on the nearby table. She is found motionless and only "stifled sobs" are heard when others are "as still as statues" (76). At this time someone from outside opens the door and asks whether the play has already started. Samant answers him by saying that the play is yet to begin. Meanwhile others try to convince Benare that it was after all a mock-trial and only a game. Unable to wake her up from her inert position Samant places the green cloth parrot in front of her and leaves. At the end of the play Benare's voice is heard singing a song softly.

The play reveals the moral hypocrisy, the sadistic tendencies, the hostility and the verbal violence of the male-dominated society against women. As a sensitive and committed writer Tendulkar perceives the harsh realities of contemporary society and depicts them artistically without preconceived notions. By using the technique of the play-within-the play, he portrays the conflict between Benare and the middle-class patriarchal society effectively. Benare who is known for her uncompromising spirit of independence and natural flavour for life has been inhumanly treated as an accused in the chauvinistic court of law. She has to undergo agonizing torture and psychological trauma for challenging the scornful and cynical social norms and mode of behaviour. She has become a desperate victim of society because she tries to live independently and enjoy life as much as possible. As an emancipated woman of modern India she has been in search of true meaning of life. Because of her motherly instinct and her care and anxiety for the well-being of her child in the womb she goes to the extent of begging the undeserving men to marry her and father her child. While she is held responsible for unwedded motherhood which is considered to be a serious act of social trespass, Professor Damle who undermines Benare's honour and self-respect by making her pregnant is allowed to go scot-free. Neither the so-called society-conscious man Mr. Kashikar nor the other members of the troupe find fault with Professor Damle who, despite having a wife and five children, has acted against the sacred institution of marriage by indulging in an extra-marital affair.

In the feminist research on women, Tendulkar has clearly disclosed in many areas of the country that the rights of women are infringed; women are exploited emotionally, socially and physically. Though Tendulkar is not a self-acknowledged feminist, he goes with the feminists in voicing women's problems. Thus, Tendulkar's dramatic world reveals his deep and uncanny insight into feminine mind. As a keen observer of life Tendulkar presents the changing reality of contemporary society authentically and honestly in the play. His real and genuine concern for the oppressed and his awareness of social evils has originated from his true understanding of society. He does not certainly approve of the waywardness of Benare but he tends to sympathize with her. Tendulkar does not offer any solution to the problem but leaves it to the discretion of the readers. Undoubtedly, Tendulkar's *Silence! The Court is in Session* carves a niche in the realm of Indian Drama in English.

Works Cited

Banerjee, Arundhati. *Introduction: Five Plays by Vijay Tendulkar,* Bombay: Oxford UP, 1992.

Gokhale, Vikram. *Ten Ani Amhi*, ed. Pradeep Mulye, Rajiv Naik, Vijay Tapas. Mumbai: Avishkar, 1992.

Ramnarayan, Gowri. "Vijay Tendulkar in Conversation with Gowri Ramnarayan." Interview. *Vijay Tendulkar's Plays: An Anthology of Recent Criticism*, ed. V.M. Madge, Delhi: Pencraft International, 2007.

Sircar, Badal. "Azad Memorial Lectures." 1982. Qtd. Ella Dutta in the "Introduction" to *Three Plays,*

Sonalkar, Sudhir. "Vijay Tendulkar and the Metaphor of Violence." *The Illustrated Weekly of India*, Nov. 18-24, 1993: 20.

Tendulkar, Vijay. "Drama: The Most Difficult, But the Most Powerful Medium." *Interviews with Indian Writers, New World Literatures Series*, B-18: 280.

Tendulkar, Vijay. *Collected Plays in Translation*, New Delhi: Oxford UP, 2003.

Tiwari, Shubha. "*Silence! The Court is in Session!*: A Strong Social Commentary." *Contemporary Indian Dramatists*, ed. Shubha Tiwari. New Delhi: Atlantic, 2007.

Sakharam Binder: A Threat to the Institution of Marriage

Tendulkar's shocking and stunning play *Sakharam Binder* is considered one of the representative plays of the Marathi theatre of cruelty. Antonin Artaud's theatre of cruelty and the angry young playwrights of Britain influenced Tendulkar to some extent who was also driven by the spectacles of human anguish. According to Artaud, theatre is like a plague. The plague signifies man's disharmonious split between the physical and spiritual force and is a vivid metaphor for the theatre. Tendulkar has quite successfully projected himself as both artist and thinker. He perceives the realities of the human society without any preconceived notions, reacts to them as a sensitive human being and writes about them in his plays as a responsible writer. He deals with gender inequality, social inequality, power games, self-alienation, false consciousness, sex and violence in his plays. The theme of violence pervades quite blatantly in most of his plays.

According to Tendulkar, the most important point is to keep the violence raw while depicting it on stage, not to dress it up with any fancy trappings, and not to make it palatable. He said that it must be acutely disturbing. He remarks:

> A torture scene must never seem comfortable. The problems arise at times because of the scale of action (on stage) for instance the mass scene in *Ghashiram.* Their experimentation with new forms became necessary. *Gidhade* was for me a tremendous release. I broke out of the frame work in which I was operating. It was shattering of the framework in which I was operating. It was shattering of the norms (Ketkat 62).

Sakharam Binder depicts the violence of the lower middle class society which is a genuine stench from the abyss, whether that abyss means lower middle class hell or the economic and sexual aggression inherent in our inequitable and repressive society. Perhaps, this was the first major breakthrough of the self-imposed confines of modern Indian drama to bring neglected areas of our common life nearer the theatre, and the theatre to be a dynamic medium (if necessary a force). Hence, we witness the stark reflections of reality, since Tendulkar seeks to demonstrate a deeper sociological and moral significance.

The success of *Sakharam Binder* largely owes to its wonderful characterization. Sakharam, Laxmi and Champa are neither characters nor schematic types. Instead they are symbols of astounding creativity. Veena Noble Dass analyzes Tendulkar's characterization:

> Sakharam is the least effective. He is seen in various roles like the ranting cock on the dunghill or a beggar for sexual favour, ending up in a moral and physical impotence. Laxmi is a superlative image of darkness and death. She begins as a scurrying refugee; she is thrown out as soon as Sakharam has exhausted her limited sexual resources. She returns insidiously and begins her drive for power. Religious rituals, calculated compassion and intrigue are her weapons. Laxmi is one of the champion life haters in drama. There is a rich interplay of ambiguity about her. Champa is a power for life, full of the rich sap. She is lewd but not lewd enough to engage in loveless sex. The disintegration and death of Champa is one of the most moving spectacles in modern drama. (104-5)

Tendulkar had been asked several times from where did this or that character in his play come? He answered that he never had one single living person in his mind as his character. He added, even if he did at the beginning the character took its own shape as it moved through the play and changed considerably in the course. The final product was a combination of many things which cannot be related to one person in real life. But many times different characteristics of different persons—known or unknown—combined automatically to form a character in his play at the very conceptual level. The incident may have been factual but the characters did not remain so. They turned themselves and the incident into fiction and the final test was how near to reality was the fiction in the play (Bandyopadhyay I).

The authenticity of the play does not lie in the roughness of the language—though one must recognize the skill with which the playwright has caught this rhythm, idiom and vocabulary of the social class without interposing any alien note, which gives it both its vitality and its freshness—but its theme is the struggle and consequently suffering that the dropouts of family and society have to undergo in order to stay alive and come to terms with life. Of these we have certain instances in the play. Sakharam is portrayed as the protagonist who turns a rebel against the hypocrisy of the men of his own class and their double standards of sexual morals. But the irony is, he is more hypocritical and more cruel than the tyrannical husbands. His exploiting and transient nature is revealed to the audience later on in the play. Sexual strength is a deceptive substitute for moral strength, whose roots he has failed to detect in his experience or psyche. Sigmund Freud in his paper entitled "Civilized Sexual Ethics and Modern Nervousness" (292) for the first time delves into the field of sociology and it is inspired throughout by warm humanitarian feeling. In this connection Veena Noble Dass applies the concepts of psychoanalysis to analyze *Sakharam Binder*: "It was in essence a protest against exorbitant demands of society, especially in the sexual sphere, on the life of the individual" (103).

Tendulkar's *Sakharam Binder* was initially banned. His depiction of a character like Sakharam who rejects the artificial values imposed by the society and the use of extremely vulgar and outspoken language incensed the censoring authorities. Later the restrictions were lifted and the play became extremely popular. Prominent actors such as Amrish Puri, Kulbhushan

Kharbanda, Sayaji Shinde, Nilu Phule, Sulabha Deshpande, Sonali Kulkarni, Sarita Choudhary and Bernard White have acted in the play.

Talking about the character of Sakharam and how it acquired a shape and life in his play, *Sakharam Binder*, Tendulkar says:

> I never met a man like him. But I was once told about a man who worked as a binder in a printing press in a small town and lived a strange kind of life. He did not marry but was on the look out for a woman who was thrown out by her husband whom he brought home and stayed with her till one of the two got fed up of the other. Then he reached her where she wished to go; gave her a pair of saris, some money and little things she would need. Then he would start his search for a fresh destitute married woman anew. His was a contract marriage without the rites. The contract ended by mutual consent. . . . It remained somewhere in my mind. . . . What kind of person could he be . . . caught my imagination. (1)

The play *Sakharam Binder* has three acts that have a definite structure that is in harmony with the development of its action. The entire story revolves around the character of Sakharam. The first act is devoted to the delineation of the relationship between Laxmi and Sakharam, while the second act portrays the relationship between him and Champa. The last act depicts the three-cornered association between the two women and Sakharam. There is, thus, a wonderful symmetry in the construction of the drama. The language used is extremely coarse, rugged, laden with abuse but at the same time crisp and colloquial. Yet the roughness of the language to catch the vocabulary of the social class is very much seen in Sakharam's words: "Damn you! What do you want? Bloody brats! You hear me? How many times have I told you? . . . You think this is some kind of *tamasha*? I'll skin your backs if you don't move on" (61), and again, "I have a foul mouth. There's always a *bidi* or an oath on my lips" (62).

The choice of such a medium for the dialogues makes the play even more alive and realistic. Thus the language of the play is as much an instrument of power and is a prolonged scream. Obscenity in language is a form of psychic violence and can be used with great effect, a weapon that can excite people to lethal physical violence.

The play, as Tendulkar has stated in an interview, grew around the central character of Sakharam, a book-binder, who though a Brahmin, is the antithesis of the general idealized conception of a member of that caste. Through the depiction of this character, Tendulkar explores the manifestation of physical lust and violence in a human being. What Tendulkar is able to achieve in his characterization, not only of Sakharam but also of Laxmi and Champa is a total objectivity. All kinds of moralizing and judgement are avoided. Tendulkar seems keen to demonstrate the basic and essential complexity of human nature which is neither black nor white but varying shades of grey. Thus all his characters are combination of good and evil, weakness and strength. This is where exactly lies Tendulkar's social realism.

Tendulkar weaves a matrix of intricate interrelationships between his characters. Sakharam, who does not believe in the institution of marriage and arranges for live-in relationships with single women who have been deserted by their husbands, shows tendencies of being religious and domesticated when in contact with Laxmi. After Champa's arrival to his house, he is transformed into a sensuous, lewd, drunkard with thoughts only of sexual enjoyment. The presence of Laxmi and Champa at the same time has a strange effect on Sakharam as if the two different modes in his character come into direct confrontation, creating a psychological disturbance in him and resulting in his temporary impotence. Champa does not foresee any possibility of competition from Laxmi when she is prepared to give shelter to Laxmi; rather she pities this homeless woman, because Champa is quite confident of her physical charms. It is this kindness of Champa only that makes it possible for Laxmi to stay in Sakharam's house. The two women between themselves share and satisfy the different needs of Sakharam—domestic and physical demands. Laxmi develops an asexual friendship with Shinde, while Champa has a sexual relationship with Dawood. Though Laxmi finds nothing wrong with her association with Shinde, her moral sense is angered by Champa's affair with Dawood and she cleverly uses this opportunity to take her revenge on Champa. This brings out the latent hatred in Laxmi for Champa. When Sakharam knows the fact of Champa's physical association with Dawood, his masculinity is doubly hurt since he himself can no longer satisfy her. Hence, in his anger, he kills Champa.

Though the characters in the play torment and destroy each other, none of the major characters indulges in self-pity. Shinde is of course an exception. But we never feel pity, rather we feel more than contempt for him. Towards the other characters we may feel compassion, but even with them there is no sense of identification. The playwright succeeds in consistently maintaining sense of distance between us and them and because too much emotional closeness might have opened up the possibility of a sentimental response. None of the characters is good as we do not wish to be like any of them. At the same time none of them is bad. We do not react to any one of them with loathing or disgust. Though we have compassion for them, with whom we have no wish to identify ourselves. This is the realism of the play.

Tendulkar is highly realistic not only in the delineation of characters and human relationships but also in the depiction of the setting in which these characters enact the drama of their lives. The locale is a mofussil town and the action takes place in a lower middle class home. The extensive stage directions, which have become more elaborate than those in either *The Vultures* or *Silence!, The Court is in Session* helps to create a vivid and detailed picture of the interior of an economically backward household. In their portrayal of this lower class of society, Tendulkar's plays signified a definite departure from the mainstream Marathi drama that mostly dealt with the more privileged sections of society. Yet, there is in this play, as in *The Vultures,* a subtle underlying tone of sensitivity and tenderness towards humanity as a whole. One can discover, if one delves into the core of the play, the seeds of basic human values. In Sakharam's playing of the *mridanga* and the joy he finds in it, in Laxmi's friendship with birds and insects and Dawood's loyalty to his friend until he is charmed by Champa's attractions. In Champa's generosity towards Laxmi, the kinder aspects of human nature and its inclination towards higher values are unfolded. The action of the play is fast-moving and packed with incidents. The complexities of situations and relationships are well handled. There is a plenty of irony in the play. There is suspense at the end of the play which keeps the interests alive. But critics have often found fault with the ending of the play.

It may be said that Vijay Tendulkar's journalistic background helps him to keep the drama strengthened where his grip never weakens, and where not a word is out of place. In fact, his inspiration comes from the society around him since he is a keen observer of human relationships, especially in lower and middle class society.

The performance of *Sakharam Binder* in 2004, a month-long Tendulkar festival in New York, proved that Tendulkar was wholly accessible to a new audience across the Atlantic. One reviewer called it the 'Spell Binder' (Ramnarayan 20). *His Fifth Woman*, a play written in English as a prelude to *Sakharam Binder*, was premiered at the festival. *The New York Times* wrote about the play:

> Sakharam's tragedy turns out to lineage on his budding social consciousness, his arrested enlightenment . . . like Brecht's *Mother Courage*; he exploits a corrupt system for personal advantage, and then discovers that the price of playing the game is everything he hoped to protect. Unlike Brecht though, Mr. Tendulkar never judges his protagonists but concentrates instead and painting him with unsetting compassion, receptiveness and thoroughness. His

play deserves to be much better known in the US than it is (Ramnarayan 90).

One of the reasons why there was such a reaction against *Sakharam Binder* was its burning naturalism. Here was a raw chunk of life with all its ugliness and crudity which was more than a shock to refined and prudish middle-class audiences. Such a direct confrontation with 'vulgar' reality was difficult for them to digest.

According to critics, "for many decades no play has created such a sensation in the theatre world of Maharashtra as Vijay Tendulkar's *Sakharam Binder*. After the production of *Sakharam Binder,* Tendulkar was accused of deliberately choosing sensational themes to get cheap publicity. He says, "Every play is not for everybody," "A play is a work of art when it reveals its theme and essence exclusively through statement and speech." (Gokhale 109). *Sakharam Binder* is probably Tendulkar's most intensely naturalistic play.

II

The play *Sakharam Binder* is divided into three acts. The first act contains twelve scenes and in all the scenes, the two characters Sakharam and Laxmi are presented, interpolated by another character Dawood Miyan. The second act contains ten scenes in which the new characters Champa and her impotent husband Fouzedar Shinde are introduced. In the second act in all the three scenes it is Champa who dominates. Even Sakharam has dominated in all the scenes in the first act, later we see Champa's dominance over him. As soon as the third act commences, the play takes a new turn with a new appearance of Laxmi at whose instance Sakharam murders Champa because of her illicit relations with Dawood Miyan.

According to Smita Mishra, "Sakharam has no social taboos. He drinks heavily, has no sense of guilt and admits to all his vices. Sakharam is a bitter critic of the institution of marriage and attacks husbands while pitying wives. He assures every woman he brings home of his 'good' treatment" (117). He frames certain rules for his women companions. He tells Laxmi who seeks shelter in his house: "you'll get two square meals. Two saris to start with and then one every year. . . . I like everything in order here. . . . I'm the master here" (125-26). By posing himself as a saviour, Sakharam never attempts to value the man-woman relationships by projecting higher moral values and tenderness onto it. Rather, he is prepared to throw out women when 'there's no spark left' in them. He brings down the man-woman relationship to the status of a contract—the contract being 'a link based on need' and 'the need ended, the link snapped.'

Tendulkar develops the character of Sakharam to expose the hypocrisies of our society in a more realistic way. Sakharam is a man without family. He lives with a woman who is deserted by her husband. His hypocrisy is seen at its peak while detesting the tyrannical husbands; he shows the same tyranny towards those women. While giving terms and conditions, Sakharam says that he must be respected in his house and he is supreme in every aspect. He says to Laxmi: "If someone calls, you're not supposed to look up and talk. If it's a stranger, you'll have to cover your head and answer him briefly. That's all. . . . But I must be respected in my own house. . . . In this house, what I say goes. Understand?" (126)

Sakharam is a peculiar caricature. As soon as he returns from the press, he drinks a cup of tea for which he orders the woman who lives with him. It is he who speaks and dominates. He does not allow the woman to have freedom of expression. His word is a law in his house which should be implemented at any cost. He has lived with six women before he brings the seventh one, named Laxmi. On reaching home, drinking a cup of tea, playing *mridanga* and enjoying *chilam* are his regular pastimes. Saying that how he is bluntly open and foul-mouthed Sakharam tells Laxmi: "I've been like this right from birth. Born naked, I was. My mother used to say, the brat's shameless. He is a Mahar born in a Brahmin home. And if I was, who's to blame? It wasn't my doing" (127).

This is a satire on the contemporary Brahmins and their way of living. Sakharam grew up like a cactus in the open. His world is an entirely different kind of world. For him the man-woman relationship is something absolutely commercial. He does not believe in the institution of marriage and he is a bitter critic of the institution of marriage and attacks 'husbands' while pitying the 'wives.' Sakharam seems to think that he has helped the helpless women thrown out by their husbands by providing them with food, clothes and a shelter. In return, he expects them to slave for him and satisfy his animal instincts. Catherine Thankamma comments: "He is not bothered by the fact that by exploiting their helplessness, he is subjecting them to a kind of prostitution" (83).

Sakharam is totally a hedonistic character who wants to enjoy life to the maximum extent possible. He says that without harming anyone one should enjoy life to the hilt. Only one should not be a liar or a fraud. It is observed that Sakharam reminds us of Naranappa of U.R. Ananthamurthy's novel, *Samskara*. Naranappa also broke every known taboo, drank liquor, and moved closely with his Muslim friend, had cast off his lawfully wedded Brahmin wife, and lived with a low caste woman. Sakharam is afraid of both the women, of Laxmi because she is a moral force and Champa because she is a sexual challenge. He needs to hear Laxmi laugh even in the midst of her pain, to give him the courage to seek his sexual rights for her. Champa, on the other hand, can only satisfy Sakharam's demands when she's drunk. That helps her forget her own self against an act in which her pleasure has never been considered. Because of this perspective, people consider Tendulkar a feminist. He shows how painful and torturous it is to indulge in loveless sex. Laxmi secretly regards Sakharam as her husband, because she cannot otherwise see herself in the kind of unsanctified union he proposes. She therefore, wears a *mangalsutra* in his name. She not only thinks Sakharam as her husband but also master and God and believes that her place is at his feet. We see in her a typical fidelity which is rooted in Indian culture practised by women, which mirrors cultural hegemony.

Laxmi is also a typical example for the dropouts of family and society at a large. Tendulkar's concern for women is seen in her character. But here is a difference between man and woman. Woman has to pay more price in Indian society when she is deserted by her family since she is dependent on man. Laxmi is thrown out of home by her husband because she does not beget any children. She seeks shelter under the roof of Sakharam. Whether Sakharam is called 'a dehumanized brutal wretch' (Pandey & Barua 33) or 'confused hedonist' (Samant 67), it is to be understood that he is nothing but a product of our dehumanizing culture and surroundings.

Tendulkar's exposure of hypocrisy in the man-woman relationships in the marital life in the traditional Indian society through this play is quite unique. He tries to analyze the complex situations of human life. The characters of Sakharam, Laxmi and Champa are the examples for three typical personalities in Indian modern society. Sakharam is treated negatively by his own parents and the feelings of his tender heart are hurt deeply. His world is an entirely different kind of world. For him the man-woman relationship is something absolutely commercial. He does not believe in the institution of marriage and attacks 'husbands' while pitying the 'wives.' Champa is an antithesis of Laxmi. She leaves her husband as she can no longer bear the sadistic torture of Shinde, while Laxmi is left by her husband for not bearing children. Champa never bothers about tradition. She is confident and courageous. Her mother sells liquor and tobacco. Fouzedar Shinde comes to the shop on a raid and sees Champa. He takes her away from her mother even before she becomes a woman. The sadistic treatment of her husband makes her not only confident and courageous, but alienated and frigid.

After beating Shinde, who comes to take her back, she tells Sakharam about the sadistic nature of her husband:

> No, I don't have heart. He chewed it up raw long ago. (Pulls herself free). He bought me from my mother even before I became a woman. He married me when I didn't even know what marriage meant. He'd tortured me at night. He branded me do awful, filthy things. I ran away. He brought me back and stuffed chili powder into that god-awful place, where it hurts the most. That bloody pimp! What's left of my heart now? He tore lumps out of it, he did. (167)

Champa is portrayed as a modern Hindu woman who struggles to establish the norms of the society at the cost of her self-respect. It might seem strange that Laxmi deserted by her husband and living with another man without entering into the bond of marriage, reminds us of Savitri thinking Sakharam as her husband. Laxmi's attitude, her clinging to the archetypal values, proves this. For Laxmi, Sakharam is her husband. When Laxmi's legal husband deliberately snaps her wedding necklace, he is not her husband in her opinion and also in the spirit of matrimony. Her *de facto* husband, as far as she is concerned, is Sakharam, who gives her shelter. Laxmi herself reveals this truth when she says the following words:

> My misfortune, I couldn't keep the man I married. For me this one was my husband. I worshipped him. Even when I was away, I'd worship him in silence every day. [Pulls out of her *choli* some *black beads strung on a cotton thread.* It is a *mangalsutra of sorts*] Look at this; I wore this in his name. I belong to him . . . if I have to die, let me die on his lap in full glory like a married woman (187).

Laxmi's character which shows fidelity towards Sakharam reminds us of Kanva Muni's advice to Shakuntala in *Abhigyana Shakuntala* about the role and function of an ideal housewife:

> As a wife, you must serve the elders in the family; must treat your co-wives as friends; even if your husband gets angry, you should

> not oppose him; you must never show pride over good fortunes; you must always be very modest and polite; a bride will be called a good wife only if she behaves so; otherwise she will be responsible for the downfall of her family name (Pandit 64).

This kind of attitude of Laxmi, towards Sakharam reminds us of a typical Hindu woman who keenly takes the role of a faithful wife: "A faithful wife, who desires to dwell after death with her husband, must never do anything that might displease him, who took her hand whether he is alive or dead" (Manu V, 147-56).

In Laxmi's point of view Champa is immoral, because she has deserted her husband. Interestingly, nobody could find fault with Laxmi for having deserted her husband. Rather she gets sympathy for what happens to her. This simplistic, yet, clear-cut distinction makes Laxmi feel very righteous and lets her consider herself chaste and Champa a cheat. Sakharam's weakness under Champa's rule is both literal and metaphorical. By the time he strangles Champa to death when Laxmi reveals to him her infidelity, his degradation has become saturated. It is the stage of his spiritual death, the death of his identity as an independent, proud and self-respecting individual. After he kills Champa, Sakharam is close to death even in a literal sense, for now his life is in the hands of law. If his crime is discovered, he will be subject to capital punishment. In this crisis, it is Laxmi who plans to save him. When Sakharam is shocked and unable to act after his murder of Champa, Laxmi cleverly utilizes the opportunity and takes the situation in her hands to support him. She suggests:

> Now don't be afraid. We'll—we'll bury her. Where do you think? Not out there—no. Somewhere here. Inside. . . . No one will suspect. I'll swear by God. He knows everything. He knows I am virtuous. He'll stand by me. He won't judge you. I'll tell Him to count my good deeds as yours. I'll do everything for you. Yes—God will forgive you. I'll tell him. He listens to me. (197)

Champa likes Dawood for his human nature and she feels endeared with him. As she finds human love more in Dawood than in Sakharam, she wants to indulge in love-making with Dawood. This is clearly seen when Sakharam becomes impotent. She is honest in what she does. Unlike Laxmi, she prefers human goodness to human tradition and unlike Sakharam, she breaks the tradition in order to be human and humane. But she can't forgive her husband because he has torn her heart. Shinde and Sakharam have tormented her body. However, she does not suffer from powerlessness as Sakharam and Laxmi do. It is through Laxmi and Champa that Tendulkar shows how deep-rooted women's exploitation in society is. Laxmi is hegemonically suppressed, used and abused. But there is no 'reversal' in her realization; still resumes continuing in the same condition with more fervour. But Champa is different.

Sakharam, though conspicuously crude, aggressive and violent, has his own laws of personal morality. He is a man who is primarily honest and frank. This openness of his personality becomes in itself a criticism of the hypocrisy of the middleclass. His straightforwardness in dealing with helpless women such as Laxmi receives a certain admiration. Laxmi, on the other hand, the replica of the ideal Indian woman, a mature version of Rama in *Gidhade*—loyal, docile, religious, hard-working, self-effacing and tender-hearted—turns out to be violent when her survival is threatened by the presence of Champa. After Champa's murder she becomes completely ruthless in covering it up than Sakharam, who is totally confused by what he has done. Champa, though coarse, shows strange kindness and generosity when she convinces Sakharam to give shelter to Laxmi who, for all she knows, may turn out to be her rival.

Among the minor characters, Champa's husband, Fouzedar Shinde, is rather interesting. There is a touch of masochism in the way he returns to Champa again and again to get abused and beaten. His friendly relationship with Laxmi shows the inherent affinity between their characters. Dawood Miyan, the only other character, is the least complex of them all. His admiration for Laxmi and physical attraction to Champa emphasizes the fundamental nature of these two women. Dawood, through his comments and observations, reveals the core difference between the relationships which Sakharam has with the two women. The four characteristics inherent in Sakharam remind us of the four conditions that are suggested by Sigmund Freud in his famous essay titled "A Special Type of Choice of Object Made by Man" (292). To be fulfilled before a man falls in love, and at first sight they appear very desperate: (1) The woman has to belong to some other man. It may happen that no attraction is felt for her until she becomes engaged or married. (2) Her reputation must not be entirely chaste. This varies from a tendency of flirtation to the extremes of promiscuity. (3) A sense of preciousness and uniqueness is attached to her in a much higher degree than is usual. (4) The man should have a constant fantasy of saving her from various imaginary dangers.

After the arrival of his seventh and eighth women Laxmi and Champa respectively into his household, there is a sea change in Sakharam's life. These two women represent two polarities of feminine response towards this sensual patriarch. When Laxmi, is thrown out of her house by her husband for not having children and is rescued by Sakharam, "She accepts the vicissitudes of life without any protest. She clings to Sakharam as her only option to survive and begins to worship her 'Saviour.' She demonstrates the patterns of thinking instilled in women by the patriarchal tradition. But Champa is boiling cauldron of fierce revolt that guts down all the men around her, irrespective of her protector or annihilator" (Burman 165). She is a woman who has deserted her alcoholic husband boldly for his cruelty perpetrated upon her. In her, Tendulkar points out that marriage is an institution in which sexual relationship for a woman is possible only if the self is forgotten in the stupor of alcohol, pleasure is possible only through inflicting pain on others. The wild, vivacious and defiant Champa's final surrender to Sakharam, after considerable resistance, shows a kind of 'compromise' or 'payment' for the shelter, food and clothing she has been offered by him.

However, with a cool business-like attitude of Sakharam, Champa uses Laxmi for the works of household and herself taking the charge of quenching Sakharam's sexual hunger. It is interesting to note how Sakharam has gradually fallen from his own position as a decision-maker. One can understand Laxmi's sympathy towards Shinde as he is her male counterpart. She cannot bear the misery of Shinde and accept Champa's deception against Sakharam. But she remains surprisingly blind to Champa's generosity towards her and the fact that Champa herself once used to be tortured by her husband. It is a flaw in the character of Laxmi in which the human element is missing as they both are sailing in the same boat.

Laxmi's discovery of Champa's infidelity towards Dawood not only gives her a sense of victory but also serves as a weapon that she can use at the crucial moment. On the other hand, when Sakharam has turned impotent, Champa finds a 'nice' substitute, in Dawood who she thinks is a good human being. Knowing his impotence which he experiences from Champa's resistance against his sexual advances, the maddened Sakharam decides to remove Laxmi forever who is a hurdle for his love life with Champa. When Laxmi is about to be kicked out of the house by Sakharam, she reveals Champa's infidelity. Sakharam, losing his balance immediately in his impotent and chaotic mental state, throttles Champa to death. After the murder of Champa, Laxmi tries her best to cover up Champa's murder and bring him out of his bewildered and shocking state and becomes his 'Saviour.' It is a pity that Laxmi, who accepts the patriarchal value system, hates Champa for betraying her husband Sakharam and sees her death as divine retribution. Such blind belief in an oppressive system appears even more stifling than Champa's infidelity.

The play ends with Sakharam's pride shattered. The bitter critic of marriage as an institution is proved, at the end, to be a staunch male chauvinist. Though he hated the tyrannical husbands, he himself is no better than them. He makes sarcastic remarks about the wives' loyalty to their despotic husbands but he himself demands complete obedience from his women. Sakharam represents the double standards of patriarchy. In the guise of 'helping' the women in distress who are in need of shelter, this man of hypocrisy indirectly throws them into a kind of prostitution.

The play is very much Indian as it reflects Indian atmosphere and surroundings. Moreover, it could have been written only by an author who knows India well, and could have been set anywhere in India. This is not because of frequent references to Indian conditions but characters and events which are an inseparable part of the play would be possible only in the Indian ethos. The play succeeds because it is able to make certain statements about life which are applicable to all people in all places. One may need to know about India in order to understand the play fully but its final effect transcends the need for this kind of knowledge and makes a universal appeal. The play has given Tendulkar a status in the theatrical world and confirmed his dubious image as the controversial playwright of our times.

According to Brijraj Singh, the disintegration and death of Champa is one of the most moving spectacles in modern drama: "The blood and guts ending of the play is a kind of theatricality to which Tendulkar has become increasingly prone. Yet the final vision—Champa's husband frantically hammering at the door, the figure of Laxmi with her claws stretching over the cowering Sakharam, digging Champa's grave is a dramatic triumph of pure evil as witnessed on the stage. That Tendulkar could suggest a cosmic clash within the drab setting of a mean house is a measure of his great talent." (39)

Indian institution of marriage has hegemonic quality in its nature. Tendulkar, through his plays, reveals that in patriarchal set up marriage not only regulates sexual reproductive behaviour and means of upholding male dominance but also victimizes both man and woman. Here in this play, Laxmi is a perfect example of victim of hegemonic patriarchy. Though Laxmi is thrown out of her house by her husband, she still considers him her god. Champa, on the other hand, is a woman of revolt. She hates her husband for the physical and sexual torture he inflicted upon her. Sakharam represents the double standards that hegemonic patriarchy sanctions. He helps helpless, abandoned women by giving shelter in his house to meet his physical and domestic needs. He does not want to be tied up by the responsibilities of the bond of marriage.

Sakharam's hypocrisy is well seen when he tries to look at unorthodox outside but stuffed with full of orthodoxical inside. He condemns Champa for drinking on the day of *Dassera*. Sakharam's wanting to do *pooja* is irony of all ironies. It is as if the roles during the Ganesh *Pooja* in the first act have been reversed! This is the social realism that Tendulkar portrays through the character of Sakharam. Sakharam is finally led to be in the hands of Laxmi. His role as the eponymous hero of the play has shifted to Champa.

The difference in the psyches of man and woman and the difference in style will result in decisions reached by consensus rather than hierarchy. In this context, General Burrows observes: "I agree . . . that man and woman are of two different psyches, and each has its own gifts to bring. I see a difference in the style of leadership. Men are more ambitious and plan ahead. Women are more involved and concerned with people. It isn't just culture-conditioning; it is their nature. I wouldn't think of myself as leading in a masculine way, which is normally aggressive and competitive. Women have more sensitivity to people and greater tolerance than men." (Edna and Wright 14)

Manchi Sarat Babu observes physical deformity in the characters of *Sakharam Binder*. (73) Sakharam's physical deformity can be seen in his alienation from parents, his bringing up and resultant behaviour and attitude towards men and women. He never bothers about people and uses women for physical pleasure. He is so cruel only because of his self-alienation, the split between his mind and body. However, finally he deforms himself mentally and morally. Laxmi is also a fine example for her belief in things. She goes to any extent for what she believes to be right. She prefers tradition which has been in vogue for ages and sacred though it has caused great suffering to all the women since its emergence. Because of the alienation of the mind and the body, she does not understand the inhuman and harmful nature of the tradition; thus she silently bears:

> I've never heard a kind word here—Always barking orders, Curses. . . . Kicks and blows. . . . There I was in agony after . . . belted, . . . all you wanted me . . . was laugh . . . laugh again. Here I am on the point of death. (148)

Tendulkar's projection of realism is seen through these women characters as they see no other alternative for them than putting up with these sufferings.

Champa's physical deformity is the result of her husband's marital rape and torture. It makes her frigid and she detests sex. However, she yields to Sakharam as she sees no alternative, "Face half a dozen animals every day! Easier to put up with this one" (18), shows how women become insecure in the society once they are out of the family. This also stresses the need of economic independence for women. This is another aspect of Tendulkar's portraying of realism.

The popular concept of marriage is that it is a union between a man and a woman. Another concept about marriage is that it is a social sanction of the union and it is accomplished by different rituals and ceremonies. Yet another view about marriage is that it is a system of roles involving primary relationships. The Hindu concept about marriage is that it is a *Samskara* or *dharma.* Marriage is one of the deepest and most complex human relationships. It is the cornerstone of a society. It involves social sanction, generally in the form of civil or religious ceremony, authorizing two persons of opposite sexes to engage in sexual union. Dr. Radhakrishnan (former president of India) observes:

> Marriage is not a mere convention, but an implicit condition of human society. It is an institution devised for the expression and development of love. Its purpose is not only the generation and nurturing of children but also the husband and wife through the fulfillment of their need for a permanent comradeship, in which each may supplement the life of the other and both may achieve completeness. (http//: www.egyankosh.ac.in/bitstream/123456789/36902/1/Unit 2.pdf.Web/15/19/2010.)

Tendulkar is a herald of human predicament. His predilection to explore man-woman relationships, especially marital, is a grand theme of his works from the beginning. As marriage plays a significant role in social discourse.

Tendulkar, as a writer, by exploring and comparing the existing familial relationships in *Sakharam Binder* with that of other plays like *Kanyadaan* and *The Vultures,* tries to establish the moulding nature of a family in the society. While other institutions have been losing their personal and local quality, the family is the one institution in our society that has become smaller and more decentralized; the only institution which retains human scale. Unhesitatingly, the play *Sakharam Binder* is not only a satire on contractual marriage system but also an attack on social hypocrisies and double standards of men in patriarchy. It exposes and explores the degeneration of family in which women are exploited to the maximum extent and become victims.

Though *Sakharam Binder* shocked the conservative society even more than *The Vultures* and is acclaimed as 'Tendulkar's most intensely naturalistic play,' the play is not without faults. One of them is that "Sakharam is very verbose and repetitive. Some of his repetitions could have been avoided without affecting his portrayal" (Dass 109). Nadkarni feels that the play is not an artistic success since it acquires a tingle of melodrama:

"It is impossible to believe that a cold and calculating man like Sakharam would rush to throttle Champa on the nearest hint of her infidelity. To murder even when angered is not so easy a task, and it is only a Shakespeare who gradually builds up the climax of *Othello* in the fashion to make it fully convincing. However, even if it is a failure it is a glorious failure." (43)

Tendulkar says that even in plays like *Sakharam Binder* and *The Vultures,* the theme is not violence. Violence comes as a way of life—a natural way of life if we consider the background of the characters. He sincerely believes that violence exists in each of us and it must be presented in all its manifestations. In an interview with Veena Noble Dass, he said, "I do not exaggerate the concept of violence, it is within us and around us." It is nothing but a reflection of social realism. The last scene of the play is characterized by the typical way of artistry of Tendulkar's playwriting. The abrupt ending of the play is connotative. Tendulkar not only portrays the bleak reality of human institution which is characterized by the suppression of truth since centuries, but also gives a call to the modern artists to be responsible exponents of the truth. However, the play exposes the greater hypocrisy in man-woman relationships in the matrix of institution of marriage which poses a severe threat to the institution.

Works Cited

Babu, Manchi Sarat. *Indian Drama Today: A Study in the Theme of Cultural Deformity*. New Delhi: Sangam, 1997.

Dass, Veena Noble. "An Interview with Tendulkar." Bombay, Unpublished, 1984.

_____. *Modern Indian Drama in English Translation*. Hyderabad: 1988.

Edna Valdez and Kim Wright. "What Men Can Learn from Women and Leadership." *Together* (Oct.-Dec. 1991): 14.

Gokhale, Shanta. "Tendulkar on his own Terms." *Vijay Tendulkar's Plays: An Anthology of Recent Criticism*, ed. V.M. Madge. Delhi: Pencraft International, 2009.

Jones, Ernest. "The Libido Theory." *The Life and Works of Sigmund Freud,* Vol. 2. New York: Basic Books, 1955.

Mishra, Smita. "An Estimation of Vijay Tendulkar as a Playwright." *Vijay Tendulkar's Plays,* ed. V.M. Madge.

Nadkarni, Dhyaneshwar. "The Case of *Sakharam Binder.*" *Enact*, no. 66, June 1972: 43.

Pandit, Maya. "Representation of Family in Modern Marathi Plays." *Vijay Tendulkar's Plays*, ed. V.M. Madge.

Ramnarayan, Gowri. "Writing for Life." *Frontline*, June, 20, 2008: 90.

Roy, Indulekha Burman. "Man-Woman Relationship in *Sakharam Binder*," *Perspectives and Challenges in Indian English Drama,* ed. Neeru Tandon. Delhi: Atlantic,

Samant, Nitin. "Tendulkar: A Confused Perspective." *Adhikar Raksha*, Jan.-June 1983: 67.

Singh, Brijraj "*Sakharam Binder*: A Reappraisal." *New Quest*. (6th Feb.) 1978: 67.

Sudhakar Pandey and Freya Barua, ed. "Casanova as the Saviour: A Study of Vijay Tendulkar's *Sakharam Binder*." *New Directions in Indian Drama.* New Delhi: Prestige, 1994.

Tendulkar, Vijay. *Collected Plays in Translation*: *Sakharam Binder*. Trans. Kumud Mehta and Shanta Gokhale. New Delhi: Oxford University Press, 2003.

Tendulkar, Vijay. *Five Plays.* New Delhi: Oxford UP, 1992.

Tendulkar, Vijay. 'The Play is the Thing.' Sri Ram Memorial Lecture I, New Delhi: Sri Ram Centre for Performing Arts. 1997.

Thankamma, Catherine. "Women That Patriarchy Created: The Plays of Vijay Tendulkar, Mahesh Dattani and Mahasweta Devi." *Vijay Tendulkar's Plays*, ed. V.M. Madge.

Kanyadaan: An Exposé of Caste Politics

As an extremely sensitive social and political problem play, *Kanyadaan* is the most controversial of all the plays written by Vijay Tendulkar, for which he once, in the most notorious display of public anger, had a slipper hurled at him. The play was acknowledged as a powerful work that explores the dynamics of caste and social change in modern India and reiterated Tendulkar's reputation as a serious thinker and gifted craftsman in the theatre. By witnessing the degree of social realism, the play is a landmark in its dramatist's career where the anti-brahmin, anti-caste and land reform movement in Maharashtra have been among the strongest in twentieth-century India, not only creating a powerful awareness within the State about the problems of untouchability and dispossession, but also mobilizing a form of reverse discrimination against the upper caste.

Tendulkar's entire process of posing the problem through *Kanyadaan* raises interesting questions. Though exogamy has been offered as a solution to the caste problem, the play also exposes degradation of human values. The play explores the human hypocrisies, cruel and sadistic nature of man and its complexities in a realistic way. Tendulkar claims to have written the play from an actual case he had seen of such a marriage. However, the present discussion focuses how the resolution of the problem leads to believe that finally the institution of marriage is sacrosanct in India, and women becoming the mere logs of wood in this sacred 'Yagna'; moreover, the question is whether women only should shoulder the responsibility to keep the institution of marriage sustained.

The play's literary reputation reached its zenith in March 1994 when it received the K.K. Birla Foundation's third

Saraswati Samman, one of India's highest literary honours, for its "effective representation of the complexity of human relationships . . . (and) the emotional connections and conflicts between the downtrodden and elite segments of society" (Saraswati Samman Award note xv). The foundation's official felicitation commended Tendulkar for creating a vibrant work that compelled intelligent readers to think, challenged their materialistic pursuits, and expressed an enduring belief in human strength and loyalty.

The play revolves around an extremely sensitive issue, the conflict between upper castes and dalits, a phenomenon still rampantly prevalent in several parts of India. Despite sixty-five years of independence, dalits continue to suffer abject misery and ill-treatment at the hands of the upper castes in some parts of India. Politicians, instead of trying to uproot this evil, seem to capitalize on it. The original vision of constitution's casteless society remains a dream since our independence. Though there are certain reasons for this, the reasons are not conspicuous. Though the issue has not been brought to the notice of modern writers on the early history of marriage, Tendulkar, with his intellectual acumen, tried his best to educate the audience on the problems of inter-caste marriages. Though the play was written in 1983, setting the story in the 1970s, the play has relevance even today.

The very title *Kanyadaan*, the father's gift of the daughter in marriage to a suitable groom, is a significant ritual within the Hindu marriage ceremony. Tendulkar's humanistic perspective that women should be treated as human beings but not as objects perhaps must have made him to take up this very theme and explore the crudities over there. The *Manusmriti*, a socio-religious compendium composed around the beginning of the era, denies women's independence (Ramabai 31). *Manusmriti* not only encourages child marriages, but also promises rich rewards in heaven for doing so. The earlier the act of giving the daughter in marriage, the greater is the merit! The girl is not only treated as her husband's property but also of the whole family: "For they [the ancient sages] declare that a bride is given to the family of her husband, and not to the husband alone" (Apastambha II) (27.3).

Once a woman is given in marriage, she must obey her husband till he is dead. A woman joined in the right way with a man also assumes his qualities, "like a river united with the ocean" (Manu ix: 22). Therefore a woman is a kind of impersonal being. She can have no merit or quality of her own. A father who demands a bride-price for his daughter unacceptably turns her into a commodity sold to the highest bidder. The best kind of marriage, instead, follows "the law of Brahma when a man dresses his daughter and adorns her and he himself gives her as a gift to a man he has summoned, one who knows the revealed canon and is of good character." (Doniger, Smith 45-46)

Marriage is a union between a man and a woman; its main purpose is not only nurturing of children but also the flowering of the personality of the husband and wife through the fulfillment of their need for a permanent bond or relationship which should be enriched with love, affection, understanding and compatibility. As marriage is one of the deepest and most complex human relationships, it is considered to be a cornerstone of a society.

The play *Kanyadaan* is said to be based on a real life incident. According to Sonalkar, the play is rumoured to be based on Namdev Dhasal's life (21). The play is about an inter-caste marriage between a dalit boy, Arun Athavale, who is a poet, and a Brahmin girl, Jyoti. But due to different family background the marriage becomes sour and the husband turns violent towards his wife. The girl goes to her parents, Yadunath Devlalikar and Seva but realizes that her place is with her husband. She realizes that Arun writes good poetry, but as a man he is worse. She accepts this crisis and goes back to her husband to live with him. There is some terrible truth in Tendulkar's play about the violence between dalit husbands and the Brahmin or upper caste wives.

Nath and Seva in their youth were political workers of the Congress Party with socialist propensities; they came to know each other in a discussion group and got married. Their political careers have gone on without any hindrance and now Nath is a legislator and Seva an organizer of women's rallies and an activist of some sort. In accordance with their political philosophy both have been championing the cause of eradication of castes from our society. As the play opens they are seen confronted with an intriguing situation; their own daughter Jyoti wants to marry Arun, a boy from the dalit community. It is a test for their ideologies now! The play is about the way they react to this and their experience of the encounter.

At the beginning of the play, we are given a glimpse of the Nath's household. The father and the mother are both rarely seen at home together because of their preoccupations: if the father is at home, the mother is away organizing rallies for women's liberation and when she returns, the father has to go out on a tour to make public speeches. Because of this parental relay-game, the children have to be at home and pass on the messages of the father to the mother and vice versa. Jyoti has to discuss the question of her marriage—a matter of life and death to her—in fifteen minutes, as the father has a bus to catch, which will take him to his speech making tour and the mother has just returned home with fatigue after a rally. This shows the quality of the family life these two social reformers have been able to give to their children, despite their observance of democratic norms. Superficially, the atmosphere in the house is liberal and democratic, the harsh fact is that the parents have really no time for their children, being involved in the public service activities. In fact, the children are seen not as individuals with their own aspirations, but as mere extensions of their parents' social experimentations. The fact about the family is the most significant one as the whole play turns upon it. Though the play was staged in 1983 for the first time under the direction of Sadashiv Amarapurkar, its relevance to the present times cannot be denied which proves Tendulkar's vision of life.

Tendulkar shows going beyond the norms of culture and tradition in marriage will only be a tragedy in a casteist society like India. He seems to pose a question: 'is marriage supposed to be for love? Or love for marriage?" And finally he proves that there is no happy ending for romantic love. Tendulkar is a realist in the sense that we can never see anywhere in his plays the happy ending of romantic love unlike most of the commercial literature. Jyoti's role reveals us that such a mutually fulfilling relationship requires an awareness of self-knowledge and a roughly accurate perception of our partner. A marriage based on romantic love will always be a failure. The ideal image that Jyoti has about Arun is 'he writes beautiful poetry and 'inspiring autobiography.' After reading some parts of his autobiography Jyoti's heart is filled with sympathy towards Arun. She feels that she could do anything for him and his happiness. The romantic love is as dangerous as sympathetic love. Love which has roots on the strong moral ground with certain degree of maturity only can survive beyond caste, creed and culture otherwise the observance of exogamy will be a daydream.

II

The play *Kanyadaan* is divided into two acts; each of which is further divided into scenes. Act I has two scenes, and Act II three scenes. As the title suggests, the play focuses on marriage—an institution which is a foundation for the super structures of family, society and nation. The marriage in the play is an unusual one which leads to complex problems—cultural, attitudinal and personal.

Though we witness a happy family gathering in the opening scene, we feel at the same time, a little disturbed as both Nath and Seva do not spend much time with their children, Jayaprakash and Jyoti. Nath is a busy man who is always on tour delivering public speeches. Seva is also busy organizing women's rallies and camps. Though it's like 'hide-and-seek' game and its further consequences in their future familial relations alarm Nath, his intention of reviewing it has not been materialized. Both Jayaprakash and Jyoti are habituated to their long periods of absence as the following conversation reveals:

Nath: Two weeks have gone by, and this hide-and-seek continues. When she goes to Bombay for a women's camp, I stay here to lecture in Poona. If she comes to Poona, I go to Aurangabad to take part in a rally for people's rights.

Jayaprakash: Don't worry, Dad! The two of us are always here. We keep conveying your messages to each other.

Nath: That's just it! Sending messages to one another cannot be called marriage. Isn't a thing called co-existence? Eh? This is all much of a rush, baba! This matter will have to be reviewed seriously sometime.

Jyoti: First the rush and scramble must stop. For both of you. (499)

This is a comment on the quality of the family life these two social reformers have been able to give to their children, despite their observance of democratic norms. The roles of father and mother in socializing with their children cannot be undermined and here we witness the utter failure of parents in doing so. Hence, the children are not seen as individuals, rather puppets in the hands of their parents. This fact has become most significant one as the entire play builds upon it.

When Jyoti declares her intention to marry a dalit boy, it creates a heated discussion at home. The parents are unnerved but they are too seasoned as politicians to show their inner unease. Seva is shocked to hear her daughter but Nath is excited and dismisses his wife's questions concerning the boy's background and occupation. They realize that now their role as public advocates of inter-caste marriages and casteless society is on test. Seva's reaction to the news displays a great maturity which presents social realism. Perhaps she may be right as a mother expressing her doubts, anticipating the problems that are to be faced by her daughter through this marriage, though she is not against inter-caste marriages. As parents' reaction is naturally cagey and guarded at first, Seva says that Jyoti is acting in haste and then she talks of the incompatibility of their life style. Two months for getting acquainted with a person is too short a period to enter into the bond of marriage. Here, Seva's prudent thinking and her experience of life, her keen observance of people have a great significance as we witness later in the play which depicts social realism.

In this play, Tendulkar exquisitely delineates how the parents' influence in realizing their dreams about certain ideals affect the life of children, making them preys to their experimentation. This is the social realism of the play we are to witness. We see how Nath is excited to hear the news of Jyoti's intention of marrying a dalit boy. He ecstatically reacts to the news. Perhaps, he starts dreaming his ideal come true through his own daughter. But he lacks practicality when he keeps aside all the doubts that are expressed by his wife Seva. Seva's questions concerning the boy's 'parents' occupation,' 'intelligence,' 'trustworthiness,' and 'life style'—show her complete vision about life and her practical thinking. It also shows a mother's natural and genuine anxiety which mirrors social realism.

In fact, incompatibility of culture and life style is precisely the general argument against inter-caste marriages. Having financial stability to enter into marriage is a must. When Seva knows that the boy does not have a job she is taken aback by the decision of her daughter. She tries to explain the real hurdles of such a marriage as marriage is considered to be a lifelong relationship. The explanation of Seva as mother seems to be not to discourage Jyoti but to let her know the practical problems involved in such a relationship and to prepare her to take a wise decision.

Actually, as a social activist Seva is not against the marriage because Arun is a dalit. Her only suspicion and fear is whether Jyoti is able to fit and adapt the culture in which Arun was nourished. It is obvious that well-educated Seva and Nath having good status of their own in the society nurtured their children in a healthy atmosphere with discipline and good culture. We see that Jyoti and Jayaprakash are well-behaved with much understanding and showing respect towards their parents. Jyoti is humble as well as sensitive. Her sense of appreciation and child-like innocence is revealed when she praises Arun's poetry and his autobiography. Her immaturity knows no bounds in nodding her head to the proposal of Arun whose motive is logical and cunning. He cleverly cashes on her innocence expressing self-pity through caste politics. The fears and anxiety of Seva are disclosed in her words: "My anxiety is not over his being a dalit. . . . You have been brought up in a specific culture. . . . He is different in every way. You may not be able to handle it" (509).

The irony of all ironies is that Jyoti nods her head simply when the boy proposes so casually as if offering some tea. When asked whether she fell in love with the boy Jyoti answers to her father:

> I don't know. Arun asked me, isn't the very idea of marrying me dreadful to you? I said, what is dreadful about that? Arun said, you don't think that I am an absolutely worthless fellow? I said, no! He said, this is incredible, and added, in that case let us get married. And I nodded. (507)

Somehow, Nath does not like Jyoti's answer. He feels as if his dreams have been shattered. He stresses again: "No surge of intense feelings in your heart? (Upon Jyoti's shaking her head.) No rainbow-hued notes played upon your nerves? (Upon her shaking her head again.) . . . (She shakes her head again.)" (507)

One will be surely surprised by the decision taken by Jyoti. Though she does not fall in love with Arun and only because she likes his poetry and is inspired by his autobiography she has made up her mind to marry him. Tendulkar shows how Jyoti is naïve in taking such an important decision about her life. Tendulkar reiterated many times that he has written what he has seen around him. There is no exaggeration in his portrayal of the characters of Jyoti and Nath. Talking about the biographical element in *Kanyadaan*, Tendulkar says: "Nath Devlalikar, the protagonist of *Kanyadaan* is me and many other liberals of my generation whom I understand completely. The pain of these today, the defeat they have suffered, the fundamental confusion and naiveté that has lead to their pain and defeat, these form the theme of *Kanyadaan,* and I wrote about it because it came so close to me." (96-97)

In spite of the candid confession about her state of mind which clearly stands in need of guidance, Nath, as confirmed later, almost pushes Jyoti into the marriage. Lacking parental affection himself, he thinks that it is a great opportunity for an ideological experiment to realize his dream. He reassures her, "doesn't matter, Jyoti, don't worry. We are all with you" (509), and leaves.

In Act I, scene ii, Jyoti invites Arun to her house to introduce him to her parents and brother. Arun is dark-complexioned and has harsh face. Yet he is good-looking. On entering the comfortable middle-class house, Arun feels quite nervous and ill-at-ease. He does not want Jyoti to leave him alone, saying "I feel uncomfortable in big house" (512). Jyoti is surprised. As the conversation goes on, Arun's eloquence on the subject of untouchability intensifies. His words spit venom. They express his hatred for Brahmins:

> Our grandfather and great grandfathers used to roam, barefoot, miles and miles, in the heat, in the rain, day and night . . . shouting 'Johar, Maayi-baap! Sir—Madam, Sweeper'! and their calls polluted the Brahmins' ears. . . . How can there be any give and take between our ways and your fragrant, ghee spread, wheat bread culture? (513)

However, from this the contrast between the soft and protected life in which Jyoti has been brought up and the harsh existence through which Arun has come becomes all the more glaring. He tells her, "Surely we can't fit into your unwrinkled Tinopal world" (513). He bluntly asks her further, "Will you marry me and eat stinking bread, with spoilt dal in my father's hut? Without vomiting? Tell me, Jyoti, can you shit every day in our slum's village toilet like my mother?" (513)

Jyoti perhaps for the first time sees his rudeness and feels the roughness of his language. She covers her face with her hands so as to hide her tears. But he goes on relentlessly, "and you thought of marrying me. Our life is not the socialist's service camp. It is hell, and I mean hell. A hell named life" (514). The rough and harsh words of Arun, obviously, make Jyoti stun with shock. Her eyes well-up with tears but she hides her face not to show them. Later, Arun, somehow, realizes that he is causing Jyoti great pain by his outburst and he apologizes to her asking her to forgive his moods for they arise out of his feeling of injustice, frustration, inner desire for revenge and his utter helplessness. This pleases Jyoti and she takes her hands off her face and smiles.

Then only Seva enters witnessing this scene. She hides her displeasure and asks Arun about his education, future prospects etc. Arun feels as if his weakness is pinpointed by Seva deliberately. He feels insulted and retorts by giving her an answer which shocks her sensibilities no end:

> Seva: It is no longer an easy thing to run a household. . . . If there is no money, there should be stable career at least. Otherwise one suffers, and the wife has to suffer for no reason.
>
> Arun: [*Patience running* out] We don't worry about such problems.
>
> Seva: You have to worry. How can anyone escape them?
>
> Arun: No problem. We shall be brewing illicit liquor. (516-17)

The rude answer given by Arun completely puts Seva down. Her reputation at the Congress Seva Dal does not come to her rescue now. The answer makes her more stiffened in her opposing the marriage of Jyoti to Arun. The battle-lines between them are clearly drawn. Arun goes on explaining the advantages of the trade of brewing illicit liquor even in the presence of Jyoti and her brother Jayaprakash; and when Jyoti tries to handle the situation, Arun shouts at her telling her to shut up. The atmosphere is quite tense to the breaking point when Nath walks in. Not knowing the situation in the house he bubbles over Arun. Later, he gives a mini-lecture on inter-caste marriage, from which it is clear that he is overjoyed by the prospective marriage not because his daughter has found a good husband but because it will fulfill his long-cherished dream of breaking the caste barriers. In other words, he completely misses the human aspect involved in the matter and is carried away by its ideological import. It is important to notice this point here for, as it turns out significant later on in the play, as Jyoti's marriage for Nath is only a means of promoting his ideological agenda.

Nath is very much enthused over his daughter's courageous decision but in supporting Jyoti to the hilt he is quite blind to Seva's objections, the significance of which for practical life can hardly be exaggerated. His blindness extends to the fact that even Jyoti is not quite sure as to why she wants to marry Arun. He brushes aside Seva and Jayaprakash's objection to the marriage for the haste in decision as "nonsense."

When Arun gets up and leaves the house without even touching the tea and snacks brought by Jyoti, the family freely discusses Jyoti's decision to marry him. It is, of course, natural that Jayaprakash and Seva are against the match, having seen and heard of Arun what they have. Even when they present their objections with concrete pieces of evidence of Arun's barbarian and rude behaviour, Nath, blinded by his ideology, brushes them all aside ascribing them to their caste prejudices and makes a plea for compassion and sympathetic understanding. He goes to the extent of even justifying the rough edges of Arun's character in the name of social justice. The difference between Seva's intensely practical view and Nath's equally intensely idealistic view becomes increasingly clear:

Nath: Look, Seva, society cannot be transformed through words alone. We have to act as catalysts in this transformation.

> The old social reformers did not stop with making speeches and writing articles on widow remarriage Many of them actually married widows. Why did they do it? . . . That was also an experiment, a difficult experiment. But they dared to risk it.
>
> Seva: Does it mean that my daughter's life is to be used for an experiment? Is that what you are saying? You may have your views. I cannot accept them. I am her mother. If you ask me I will say that Jyoti can never be happy with that man. (524)

When the parents have a great difference of opinion as evident in their continuous argument over her marriage, the decision is left to Jyoti, who is also not very clear about her own feelings. When pointedly asked about her opinion of Arun, she can only reply:

> (diffident, immersed in thought) Bhai, I told you at the outset. . . . I don't know much about him . . . he asked me, I said yes, quite spontaneously. . . . And sometimes such a different side, that it strikes me, I don't know him at all. At times I feel I can trust him, but at the very next instant I am left miles behind him. I ask my self—this thing that I want to do, is it the right thing? (524-25)

As Jyoti is still in confusion and dilemma, Nath asks her the usual questions about her being aware of the consequences of her decision and so on. When she answers more out of sense of duty rather than out of conviction, the matter is closed for him and as per the democratic traditions of the house, one must forget one's differences of opinion and stand by Jyoti. Seva's pointing out that a house cannot be run like the office of a political party doesn't much impact Nath. But Seva firmly announces her "party rebellion" and sticks to her guns. Now, Nath gives the family a lecture on social justice; and for him Jyoti's marriage is not so much a matter of the coming together of two persons in flesh and blood. It is not a marriage of two minds but of two ideological abstractions! It is on this high moral, idealistic note that the first act ends. The stage direction says that darkness descends at the end of Nath's speech, which is symbolic in more than one way. It signals not only the confused state of the household but also warns the future storm in which the family is going to be faced after this marriage of two ideologies.

Some months pass by between the first and second acts. Jyoti not only marries Arun but also returns home after her first taste of married life. She is a 'beaten' figure in every sense of the term. Seva's fears have come true. Arun has no room of his own and hence the couple has to spend their nights in some friend's house or another's; they find it difficult to get a house for them; every night Arun comes home in a drunken state and beats Jyoti. Unable to bear this physical and mental torture any longer, Jyoti decides to spend her nights alone in her maternal home. As the second act begins we learn that Jyoti decides never to go back to Arun. Because of Arun's inhuman treatment of Jyoti, her marriage is on rocks. When Nath learns of Jyoti's tales of woe, he suggests that Jyoti and Arun should come to stay with them rather than wander from one friend's house to another's. He states Arun's ill-treatment of Jyoti as a result of the harsh environment in which he has been brought up; if he gets a better surrounding, such as Jyoti's maternal home, he will definitely improve. Jyoti rejects the offer outright, saying that she has come home for good. Nath, earnestly appeals to Seva to see to it that the marriage does not fail. Still, the marriage for him is an ideological experiment:

> [*With passion*] Seva let not this wonderful experiment fail! This dream which is struggling to become real let it not crumble before our eyes! We will have to do something. We must save this marriage . . . this is not just a question of our daughter's life, Seva this has . . . a wider significance . . . this experiment is a precious experiment. (537)

Out of sheer ambition of saving the marriage of his daughter, Nath is unable to see the psychological damage that is being done to his daughter.

Now, Arun, as if realized, not only rings up but comes home to say sorry to Jyoti. Exhibitionistically, he declares his love for her; when Seva asks him why he beats her, he tells her to look at his love and not at his beating! Soon an argument develops between them about who is in the right and who is in the wrong. But Jyoti, in order to stop the whole show, declares her intention of going back to Arun this time forever. Seva is against this continual folly and stubbornness of Jyoti. But as Jyoti goes away, Nath feels happy and says to Jyoti: "Jyoti, I feel so proud of you. The training I gave you has not been in vain" (541). But he too is not completely happy after what he has seen and heard; he perhaps, for the first time prays to God for the well-being of Jyoti.

Between the first and second scenes, a few more months elapse. In the latter scene, the ideological scales finally fall off Nath's eyes. As the scene opens we find him going through and admiring his dalit son-in-law's recently published autobiography. Seva returns from the hospital where the pregnant Jyoti has been admitted after her being brutally beaten and kicked by Arun in the belly. When Nath learns this, he fails to understand and explain Arun's behaviour. For one thing, it goes against his cherished principles and his ideological dream seems to be crumbling. For the first time he confronts the inhuman element involved in his social experimentation. As he sits confused and wonders as to how a person who himself has gone through so much suffering can inflict pain on others, Seva explains the situation with a proper reason. The reason is that Arun does not want to work. He wants to remain a burden on Jyoti. Obviously, he will never feel grateful for her support also. This is a satire on the writers of autobiographies that reflect hypocrisies. When Nath warns her about her harsh words, she still continues her analysis:

> You can't stop me . . . the truth is that your dalit son-in-law, who can write such a wonderful autobiography, and many lovely poems, wants to remain an idler. . . . He wants his wife to work. And with her money he wants to drown himself in drink, and have a hell of a time with his friends. On top of that, for entertainment, he wants to kick his wife in the belly. Why not? Doesn't his wife belong to the high caste? In this way he is returning all the kicks

> aimed at generations of his ancestors by men of higher caste. It appears that this is the monumental mission he has set out to fulfill. (543-44)

Nath, perhaps, for the first time realizes his folly in promoting the match of Jyoti and Arun. His liberal view of Arun slowly starts getting changed to a realistic one. He declines an invitation for speaking at a seminar organized on Arun's book. His opinion of the son-in-law receives a further jolt when Seva informs him about the statements Arun is reported to have made about his in-laws. Nath finds all this behaviour of Arun hard to digest, but then in comes Jayaprakash with the newspaper report about the harassment of Palestinians at the hands of the Israelis. The discussion that follows on victims/victimizers helps to put Arun's behaviour in a perspective that Nath can understand. The discussion serves to bring out the fact that in the name of different versions of justice in our times—racial, social and gender—new false ideologies are replacing the false ideologies of the old; how can one call this state of affairs an improvement on the past? It has been Tendulkar's firm belief seen throughout his plays from *Silence! The Court is in Session* to *Ghashiram Kotwal,* that violence is an innate part of human nature. Nath confesses that he too feels anger for what Arun says and does. Gosavi observes: "after all, he is no Mahatma, but still hypocritically clings on to civilized norms as demanded by his ideology" (163).

As if to put Nath's ideology to further test, Arun visits him with two of his friends, Hameer Rao and Vamanseth. He has come to inform Nath that presuming his acceptance; they have arranged discussion on his autobiography with Nath as the chairperson. The invitation is really a form of blackmail. Nath burns with inward anger for the man who daily beats and kicks his daughter and yet who has the guts or shamelessness to invite her father to speak on his book. But, he, in his own polite way, sends them away regretting his inability to accept their invitation. The invitation is really a trap for Nath: if he declines it, Arun can propagate him as a casteist and thus damage his public image; if he accepts it, he has no option but to praise the book. Nath, however, has courageously chosen the first option. But Seva warns him that such a course of action will cast their daughter still in unforeseen troubles. This time Nath decides to follow Seva's pragmatic advice as it accords well with his public pronouncements.

In the final scene, we see Nath returning home after chairing the discussion on Arun's autobiography. He has made a glowing speech, showering accolades on the book, though inwardly he was cursing it and its author. All this he had to do to preserve his progressive image in the public and also to ensure that it spares his daughter from getting beaten. For the first time perhaps he has said what he did not feel at heart. He breaks down completely by the painful awareness of his utter helplessness in the matter which forces him to carry this hypocritical task so repugnant to him. Moreover, he is further troubled by the fact that Jyoti had come out of the hospital to attend his performance.

After coming home, Nath condemns the book as an artistic hoax. The autobiography, if it is in the form of literature, is expected to be a replica of facts unlike fiction. But Arun's book is a pack of lies. Incidentally, what Nath says publicly about the book and what he says at home is symbolic of the way of similar dalit autobiographies in Maharashtra being treated by scholars and leaders of Nath's persuasion. After his own experience of suffering at the hands of Arun himself, he now realizes how he has made his own daughter a prey to his idealism. He rolls down into pain reminiscing his encouragement and uncompromised support for Jyoti in marrying Arun. He now realizes how he was unable to pay attention towards the warnings of his wife in his over-enthusiasm to uproot casteism from society. But in his maniacal urge, he pushed his own daughter into a sea of misery. With the self-knowledge of Nath in the form of repentance makes him completely down. In response to the remark made by

Jayaprakash that he has sounded tired during the ceremony Nath replies:

> You are mistaken. That was the lump which came to my throat when I read Arun Athavale's masterpiece. I deliberately managed to sound hoarse. I picked the most beautiful words in the language and murdered them as I flung them at the public. I distorted the words of great men and reduced them to dust. Byron and Kusumagraj are poets very dear to our hearts. I cheerfully strangled them. At one time, how deeply we had been influenced by Khandekar's maudlin idealism. Today, wherever he is, Khandekar must be turning in his grave. Today I used even him. Why? . . . For the sake of my precious daughter, my innocent child. If she has committed any crime it is this: she took her father's values. She was guided by her father's humanism and liberalism. (558)

Here, Nath's words which are full of agony and pain reflect the hypocritical speech he has made at the ceremony for the sake of his daughter. He has strangled his idealism to the blackmailing of Arun, against his will. This is the realism of the play.

At this moment only Jyoti enters. She has been a severe critic of his speeches right from her childhood and now she has come to get an answer to a basic question. She has nothing to say about the speech itself for she knows it to be all false. She wants to know why Nath chaired the discussion. She discovers as she had suspected that it was ostensibly to spare her suffering more rather than out of any genuine admiration for the book. And the discovery is a shattering one for Jyoti, for it destroys the image of her father as an uncompromising idealist. Now she knows that by his hypocritical and insincere participation in the discussion, Nath was compromising on his ideology which she finds unable to digest. For this ideology only, she with full trust in her father, not only marries Arun but also resolves to go back to Arun when she faces crisis in her married life. Now, slowly, she starts knowing her father's real form of ideology. In short, Jyoti now realizes that his ideology and his public image were far more important to her father than his own daughter and that she has become a mere pawn on his ideological chess-board.

Through the discussion between Jyoti and Nath, Tendulkar rules out the philosophical school of thought that man is innately good and violence is a result of the circumstances in which he is nourished and can be changed through the change of environment. Clinging to this philosophy the idealistic parents like Nath do not foresee the damage done to their children. Jyoti finds out from her questioning the true reason behind Nath's making a speech on Arun's book and rebukes him for his insincerity. "Your speech today was not only lousy; it was a hireling's speech" (562). To her question why he praised the book when he did not like it and hated its author, Nath simply denies that he hates Arun by taking recourse to the Gandhian doctrine 'hate the sin, not the sinner.' As someone engaged in the task of implementing that philosophy, Jyoti asks Nath: "Yeats writes at the end of his 'Among Schoolchildren'—how do we know the dancer from the dance?" (Gosavi 166)—How to separate the sinner from the sin because they form one indivisible totality. Jyoti cries in pain:

> I grew up listening to such talk day in and day out. . . . No man is fundamentally evil, he is good. He has certain propensities towards evil. They must be transformed. Completely uprooted and destroyed. . . . It is essential to awaken the god slumbering within him. . . . All false and vicious claptrap! The truth is, you knew very well that man and his inherent nature are never really two different things. Both are one, and inseparable. And either you accept it in totality, or you reject it if you can. . . . Putting man's beastliness to sleep, and awakening the godhead within him is an absurd notion. You made me waste twenty years of my life before I could discover this. I had to learn it on the strength of my own experience. (563)

Tendulkar's message that 'man and his inherent nature are never really two different things, both are one and inseparable' through this play receives a tremendous response.

Though Jyoti has learned this truth from her own experience it is an expensive one which she did it at the cost of her own life. Referring to her own specific case Jyoti poses the question as to how to separate the evil Arun from the good one, for he is both the passionate lover and her evil tormentor. If she accepts him at all, it has to be *in toto*. Jyoti asks her father in agony: "Arun is both the beast and the lover. Arun is the demon . . . the poet . . . bound together, one within the other, they are one. . . . Tell me where is that beast I should drag out and destroy." (564)

Nath, out of belated parental affection, reassures her of his support if she chooses to come back to him. But it is too late. Jyoti brilliantly checkmates him by throwing one of his favourite ideas in his face:

> It will not happen, Bhai, because you yourself have taught us that one must not turn one's back upon the battlefield. It was you who always taught us that it is cowardly to bow down to circumstances. . . . This drug Bhai has entered and mingled with our blood. The poison has numbed our entire consciousness. We cannot run away . . . and continue to lose our lives as guinea pigs in the experiment. (564-65)

After this philosophical demolition, Jyoti goes on to reject Nath as father by telling him of the permanent psychological damage he has done to his children. Jyoti firmly decides to dissociate with her family forever. As a married daughter she reminds her father: "(harshly) I have my husband. I am not a widow. Even if I become one I shan't knock at your door. . . . Now, I am Jyoti Arun Athavale, a scavenger" (566). These last words of the play nearly sum up Jyoti's rejection of Nath as her philosopher and guide and more painfully as her father. It is often said that in a marriage a father loses his daughter, but in Nath's case the Kanyadaan—giving away of the daughter—has been doubly painful, in his giving away Jyoti to Arun he has lost her in more ways than one. His Kanyadaan has turned out to be a sacrifice of his daughter on the altar of his socio-political ideology.

The violence which is shown in the play is real. And does one excuse such violence because it is a kind of revenge against centuries of anti-dalit violence? This is the most disturbing aspect of the play. In this play, Tendulkar uses violence in a different way. It raises all kinds of questions including the correct paths of improvement of the state of life of the oppressed. It raises questions even about violence and non-violence as means of social change, the dimension of male violence against women is not excluded. What one does not quite understand, however, is the daughter's last speech. Jyoti is portrayed as a typical Hindu wife prepared to face her husband whatever be circumstances she is placed in. She acts the way she does, because she still feels a sense of social guilt. She accepts violence as a way of life. Despite the ambiguities in her outlook the girl is not confused at all, and seems to have grown to hate her father who with all his Gandhian principles seems to have taught the wrong thing about life and misguided her. The question is not whether all dalit men are like the one who is portrayed in the play. The question is about the utter painful and confusing task of reforming our wretchedly unjust and increasingly violent society.

Tendulkar moulds the protagonist Jyoti's character as a tragic heroine who suffers because of *hamartia.* Despite all her mother's warnings she decides to marry Arun, just because she likes his poetry, within two months of familiarity with him.

The last words of the play are an indictment over the failure of exogamy in caste-based society. Jyoti's frustrated expression "We shall continue to lose our lives as guinea pigs in the experiment" (565) is an indirect verdict declaring the tragic end of inter-caste marriages. Among the few protagonists in contemporary Indian theatre, male or female, who assert their will in order to alter their condition, Jyoti stands different because she chooses a worse life, not to continue it but to change it? Veena Noble Dass observes that the image of woman in contemporary Indian literature has changed drastically. She observes: "No more is woman considered or portrayed as a weak person, or falling at the feet of her husband or trying to please him always. . . . Modern writers have tried to transform this image of woman as seen in the myths by portraying them in a more realistic manner. One such writer is Vijay Tendulkar" (11).

Benare in *Silence! The Court is in Session* does not kill herself or feel shy for whatever has happened to her and continues her fight till the end. Rama, in *The Vultures,* does not believe in her fate but would do anything to change her life. Champa and Laxmi in *Sakharam Binder* are two life forces to question the male chauvinism. Kamala opens the eyes of Sarita in *Kamala,* and resolves to live the life of human than marital slave. Here, in *Kanyadaan,* Tendulkar takes a different turn of moulding the character of Jyoti evoking many questions. Being economically independent, unlike other women characters of Tendulkar (Benare is an exception) Jyoti neither thinks of giving divorce nor resolves to go back to her parents, but decides to uphold the sacred institution of marriage in terms of Indian culture.

When Jyoti thinks she is betrayed by her father and becomes a guinea pig for his experiment, the repentant Nath offers her a chance of rectifying his mistake. But Jyoti outrightly denies his proposal, and prepares to go back to her husband. Why does she not think of living independently, ruling out the idea of going back to her sadistic husband is a million dollar question. She may at least think of her fellow women who have been victims suffering ages together at the hands of their tyrannical husbands, and resolve to change their lives by making them aware of their social condition. In the play *Kamala* Sarita expresses a hope and assertion not to continue as a slave to her husband Jaisingh, but to change his attitude. But here in *Kanyadaan,* we see Jyoti's miserable end by becoming victim of her father's ideology. Though, Jyoti suffers because of *hamartia,* her bold decision of continuing with her husband to uphold the sanctity of the institution of marriage purifies the audience's mind. By preparing herself to face the music, Jyoti says: "even if running away was the general rule of conduct, we shall continue to recite 'March on, Oh soldier!' Hence Jyoti becomes a 'guinea pig' in the ideological social experiment of a social reformer, who is naïve and blind to truth.

Thus, Tendulkar, in his play, *Kanyadaan*, not only mocks at Gandhian leader's pronouncements but also a drunken dalit poet who cashes in on his underdog status. The play is unhesitatingly, an expose of caste politics.

Works Cited

Doniger, Wendy, Brain K. Smith, trans. *The Laws of Manu*. London: Penguin, 1991.

Gosavi, Nutan. "*Kanyadaan:* An Expose of Political Progressives." *Vijay Tendulkar's Plays: An Anthology of Recent Criticism*, ed. V.M. Madge. Delhi: Pencraft International, 2009.

K.K. Birla Foundation's Third Sarasawati Samman Award Note. *Kanyaadaan*. Mumbai: Popular Prakashan, 1994.

Dass, Veena Noble. "Women Characters in the Plays of Tendulkar." *New Directions in Indian Drama*, ed. Sudhakar Pandey and Freya Barua. New Delhi: Prestige, 1994.

Ramabai, Pandita. *The High-Caste Hindu Woman*. Bombay: Maharashtra State Board for Literature and Culture, 1981.

Sonalkar, Sudhir. Qtd. Veena Noble Dass, *Modern Indian Drama in English Translation* (Hyderabad, 1988).

Tendulkar, Vijay. "Natak Ani Mee." *Selected Writings on Theatre of Tendulkar*. Thane: Dimple, 1997.

_____. *Collected Plays in Translation: Kanyadaan*, trans. Gowri Ram Narayan. New Delhi: Oxford University Press, 2007.

The Manusmriti, Apastamba II, 10, 27.3.

Ghashiram Kotwal: A Treatise on Power

Vijay Tendulkar's *Ghashiram Kotwal* is the most controversial of all the plays written by him, yet it is the most popular owing to the issues, social, political and religious touched upon in it by the playwright. It was translated into English by Jayant Karve and Eleanor Zelliot. It can be said unhesitatingly that the spirit of the original play has successfully been captured by the translators, for the tempo of the language, diction and tone could completely be maintained.

The play was first performed on 16 December 1972 at the Bharat Natya Mandir, Poona, by Progressive Dramatic Association of Poona. Between 1972-73, the play won numerous awards at the Maharashtra State Drama Competition. However, the President of Progressive Dramatic Association imposed a ban on the play after nineteen performances. He enumerated the following three reasons for banning the play. 1. It was anti-Brahmin. 2. The character of Nana Phadnavis as conceived by the playwright was historically not correct. 3. There was a fear of revolt in the audience and a strong possibility abused by the audience if the performance was allowed to continue. There was an immediate protest from the actors of the Progressive Dramatic Association. Most of the actors resigned. As a result the play was revived on 11 January 1974. It has ever since been performed extensively both in India and abroad by the actors of the Progressive Dramatic Association.

Whether Tendulkar's play is based on social realism or a historical legend is a debatable issue. Its significance lies not in its depiction or distortion of the reality. In this connection Tendulkar's words are quite apt: "The play is not historical but is cooked in somewhat historical kitchen. It goes against the integrity of a creative piece of writing to be called historical and historical into mythological. The story is not so important as what it signifies" (Bandyopadhyay iv).

According to history, Ghashiram Kotwal was a North Indian Brahmin, a resident of Aurangabad, who was appointed as the police Prefect of Poona on 8 February 1777 and continued to hold office till his death which took place on 31 August 1791, under violent circumstance (Govind 250). He had earned Nana's confidence by his faithful service during the critical times that followed the Peshwa Narayan Rao's murder. He enjoyed the full trust of Nana Phadnavis and his administration was notoriously worse than that of his predecessors. He was appointed to watch the movements of Raghunath Rao and his family. But he reported to Nana whatever suited his purpose. Due to the harassment of innocent men by his unnumbered unscrupulous spies, Ghashiram's name has become a synonym for oppression and tyranny in Poona. Tendulkar had used this piece of history for his play *Ghashiram Kotwal*. As it happens so often with a work that questions contemporary values and phenomena from a radical position, Ghashiram has been attacked on peripheral counts rather than on its basic assumptions. Tendulkar has been attacked for having shown Nana Phadnavis, a cult hero, in an unsavoury light. But the play is not really about Nana, the late eighteenth century Marathi Machiavelli who was the Peshwa's Chancellor in Poona, the Royal Deputy's deputy—but a deputy who "no longer owes his position so much to solid popularity of military backing as to the diplomatic address with which he can play one party off against another" (Bandyopadhyay iv).

In his reply to Samik Bandyopadhyay whether he really conceived the play as a study on power games or as an exposure of Brahmin corruption and hypocrisy, Tendulkar replied: "Broadly speaking I had in mind the emergence, the growth and the inevitable end of the Ghashirams; also those who create, and help Ghashirams to grow; and the irony of stoning to death a person pretending that it is the end of the Ghashirams" (Bandyopadhyay v).

What makes Ghashiram stand out from the usual Marathi plays is the fact that Tendulkar has given birth to a new self-sustained and scintillating stage form which makes the play an unprecedented achievement. The play is clearly based on certain episodes in the life of Nana Phadnavis, one of the major architects of Peshwa supremacy during the decline of Maratha Empire. Tendulkar portrays him as a leader with an overpowering weakness for young Brahmin girls of Poona. The burden of the play develops with Nana's encounter with Ghashiram, a Brahmin whom the Poona orthodoxy treats as an outsider.

Nana is infatuated with Ghashiram's young daughter Lalita Gauri—prompted by a desire to avenge the humiliation he suffers at the hands of the city's Brahmins, Ghashiram agrees to play Nana's game. By procuring his beloved daughter to old Nana's lechery, Ghashiram wants to grab the position of Kotwal. Nana makes him Kotwal of the city and gradually Ghashiram unleashes his vendetta against those very Brahmins who had once treated him like vermin. In unfolding these events which have some basis in history, Tendulkar paints an explosive picture of the moral decadence of the Poona Brahmins during the decline of the Peshwa regime. The playwright has created his own theatrical reality and is completely guided by his own organic laws.

Tendulkar has succeeded to turn it eminently theatrical since he has experimented with the dialogue and acting of the play by going against the regular traditional moulds of Marathi theatre. His unique imagination and invention has resulted in a variety of functionally effective forms such as mime, dance, music and dialogue in verse—all invested with apt folk association which Tendulkar has used innovatively: "He has blended this mixture with an artistic touch which is incomparable in the annals of Marathi theatre" (Nadkarni 73-74). During the last two decades particularly, Indian theatre has gone back to indigenous folk forms which are different from Western theatrical expression and yet relevant to our times. This urge for a fresh outlook in theatre has found wide expressions in many languages including Bengali, Manipuri, Marathi, Gujarati, Kannada, Malayalam and Hindi. A number of talented younger playwrights, directors, actors and designers have begun groping for a new vocabulary, for new styles and forms in their specific regions: "It was in the 1960s and 70s that the urge to find a new and specifically Indian theatrical language acquired urgency" (Bhalla 67). This urge has mainly been directed towards exploring the traditional and folk forms of our theatre or alternatively Sanskrit theatrical traditions with all its possibilities for imaginative productions.

To create a new kind of dramatic structure modern playwrights have used elements from traditional folk forms. Tendulkar's *Ghashiram Kotwal* falls into this group. According to Abrams:

> Some of the elements that find expression in these plays are imaginative, nonrealistic treatment of time and space, including simultaneous action, the miming of properties, objects and situations, a blending of the realistic with fantastic, the use of poetry, song, music, dance and other forms of stylized speech, gesture and movement, making the human actor an instrument of scenic design or scenic change, the use of masks and mask-like make-up, creating social prototypes rather than individualized characters, the introduction of Sutradhar, the Bhagawat or the narrator. (Dass 115)

The unique dramatic folk form employed in *Ghashiram Kotwal* is the most significant feature of the play. It has no precedence in the history of the modern Marathi theatre. The modern Marathi theatre has drawn heavily on the theatre traditions of the West, on the creations of Shaw, Moliere, Ibsen and other playwrights. But in turning to the West for inspiration it tended to ignore a variety of dramatic forms which had for centuries held an appeal for Marathi-speaking people and which had been nourished and sustained by their support and patronage. These indigenous Marathi folk forms were dismissed as rustic and meaningless. Renu Juneja says: "In fact, these forms represented a folk tradition which had in it a tremendous potential of dramatic expression. The Marathi-speaking world had been creating its own dramatic universe, through various forms like the Gavlana, the Tamasha, the Dashavatar, the Bharud, the Kirtana, and various folk songs. The rich and colourful world which was mirrored in these forms fulfilled the people's needs for dramatic entertainment" (41). Veena Noble Dass rightly observes: "But till quite recently Marathi playwrights conducted themselves as though they had nothing whatsoever to do with these forms and acted accordingly. There was an urgent need for some positive thinking on the methods by which these genuinely indigenous forms could be pressed into the service of modern Marathi theatre" (116). This task has been accomplished by Tendulkar's *Ghashiram Kotwal* which is an effort to re-create the spirit of folk theatre without diluting contemporary appeal. The thematic content is easily adapted to the folk form. The playwright himself said so, when asked why he had chosen the folk form for this play. The plot has been chosen for its symbolic overtones and not because it offers opportunities for vigorous action or realistic reaction of a slice of life.

The plot does not recall either myths or folk tales. The story of Ghashiram and Nana Phadnavis belongs to recent Peshwa history. However, the historical element has little importance as Tendulkar explains; he is merely using history to depict a recurring human and social condition. The historical background serves him well because it frees him from any obligation to render his social analysis in naturalistic terms. The historical events are sufficiently remote to allow for a symbolic heightening, especially since this segment of history has fascinated Marathi mind, often taking a larger than life dimensions. Hence, Tendulkar's choice of the 'Tamasha' framework is particularly appropriate because it offers possibilities and sanctions for a non-realistic treatment of time and place, plot and character. The historical plot and the folk conventions do not affect the contemporary appeal of the play, for its theme, how society corrupts, uses, and then discards individuals, will certainly engage and interest the modern theatre-goers.

The dramatist has his narrator anticipate and suggest plot development, thus deliberately setting aside all audience interest evoked by a clever, suspenseful plot. In allowing the Sutradhar to narrate what happens in the interval between Ghashiram's appointment as Kotwal and his ultimate exercise of power, Tendulkar frees himself from composing and bridging scenes and is able to focus exclusively on the significant point of Ghashiram's career. Although the plot is episodic, it is never disjointed. The overlooking exits and entrances characteristic of whole drama provide a scene of fluid motion and continuity. The continuous presence of Sutradhar on the stage also provides the necessary link between various episodes. Sutradhar serves other traditional functions as well. In leading the Ganesh puja with which the play begins, it manifests a ritualistic authority associated with temple priests and also signals his non-western approach to theatrical activity. The audience participates as a group, not as an individual. The Brahmins who form the human curtain first approach the stage as if from within the audience. Often Sutradhar addresses the audience directly by which the dramatist is deliberately destroying theatrical illusion. Jabbar Patel explains in his Preface to *Ghashiram* that when Ghashiram addresses the audience the effect is not alienation. Ghashiram's remarks have not interrupted the progress of the story, nor have they undermined the emotional involvement of the audience that is brought closer into the experience of the play.

Since the Sutradhar frequently describes the setting and the characters, the stage can be largely free of scenic display. As in folk theatre, the play uses very few stage properties. The naked stage allows the dramatist to telescope time and space, to simultaneously present more than one locale. The shifts in time and space are fluid. Freed of the burden of stage properties, the actors easily manipulate the space to represent different interiors.

At one point they mime plucking fruits in a garden, at another they act out the breaking of a prison door. There is no visual break between the scenes. The actors do not leave the stage, nor do they move very far away from their earlier stage position.

Tendulkar's human curtain is a radical innovation for the modern urban stage: "The difference between the western stage and the stage of Tendulkar is most spectacularly evident in the use of curtain as a theatrical device" (Bandyopadhyay vii). In a production note, the Theatre Academy says:

> The basic structure of the play is human wall which is basically a singing chorus, impersonally commenting on the episodic developments. But it also breaks into smaller tableaux, grouping and regrouping endlessly. The human wall ceases to exit when its back is turned to the audience. The Sutradhar or narrator interposes in the proceedings to keep the audience abreast of things, the actors switching parts with perfect timing. A fact of opera with verse, music and prose fusing into one another in a strange compelling alchemy. The ballet blending with the traditional folk dances sets the mood and tempo of the decadent and bawdy era (Bandyopadyay vii).

The human wall serves as an excellent symbol of the mechanism of secrecy, hiding and revealing happenings by human devices. It is the wall again that the singing chorus uses for the chant of saints' and gods' names as yet another screen of complacence and consolation reflecting the contemporary yawning horror of corruption and tyranny. While the tortured Brahmin groans, the Brahmin line chants the god's name and drowns his screams. Institutionalized sexuality and institutionalized religiosity are brought together into an unholy image of Bavanakhanni, the red light district, turned to the pleasure garden of the Krishna. "Bavanakhanni, Madhura, Avatharli-Mathura descend on Bavanakhanni." Still the sheer thrill of the musical does to a certain extent weaken the thrust of the satire and the sting is blunted. Tendulkar himself admitted:

> The criticism has a point. Even when the sting was felt in Maharashtra. The Delhi production (done by Abhiyan in Hindi) had a somewhat different impact. It had 'less entertainment value' i.e., less music, and more impact as a serious play . . . the musical form has advantages and disadvantages like other forms. I could not think of an alternative when I had to write the play. The form had certain inevitability (Bandyopadyay vii-viii).

Tendulkar was not trying to create memorable individuals. He has set out to certain universal human or social conditions. His need is best served by the type of stock characters we find in folk drama. He makes special efforts to dissociate his Nana of history. By making Nana dancing on the stage on his first appearance Tendulkar shocks his audience into considering Nana as a symbolic representative rather than as a dignified austere ruler of most historical accounts.

Tendulkar attempted to portray the character as a flat, two-dimensional without allowing it to acquire any roundedness. The attempt was to project before the audience not Nana Phadnavis the individual, but to portray him as a type of the class of statesman to which he belonged. This is the social realism of the play. And this attempt on the whole turned out to be a success. Nana's manner of speech and his gait have a rhythm which is entirely in harmony with that of the other characters. In portraying the character of Nana, Tendulkar attempted to blend it smoothly with the world of song and dance that he sought to create.

The musical composition used in the play has a distinctively folk rhythm; it is derived from the Marathi 'Tamasha.' As in the Tamasha he uses 'Lavani' to bring a sensuous, passionate element into his play to highlight important episodes (Kulkarni). Tendulkar, however, never uses the 'Lavani' to merely titillate the audience. For instance, erotic element of Ghashiram's first Lavani with Gulabi is not merely dramatically appropriate but also an indirect comment on the prevailing social corruption. The songs sung or tunes hummed by the choral figures either comment on the action or help establish the appropriate mood.

The use of music does not make this play operative in the western sense because the music exists only to highlight emotion or express mood, never for its own sake. Stage business like a corpse getting up on the way to the pyre, dwarfish Brahmin himself sitting in place of the image of Ganapati, the use of the erotic words from a Lavani to accompany the music of the devotional *Kirtan* makes the performance of the play a memorable one.

Vijay Tendulkar combines the ready wit of the Tamasha with the mime and music of the Dashavatar plays. The Dashavatar was performed in Konkan and Goa after harvesting. The folk-dance-drama is based on the ten incarnations of Vishnu, namely Matsya, Kurma, Varaha, Narsimha, Vaman, Parshuram, Ram, Krishna, Buddha and Kalki. The stage was wooden, about two feet high and there was always a single set. The theme portrayed was the destruction of evil. The chief actor was the Haridasa, always very colourfully dressed, flanked on either side by two disciples. And behind him stood a chorus in half circle. The Sutradhar informally introduced the drama. The speeches were mostly extempore. With the entry of the demons, colour powder was thrown and there was much noise and jumping and brandishing of swords. The musical accompaniment was the Mrudanga and the Jhanza. The Tamasha was performed by a roving troupe of about seven to eight actors comprising a dancer, a comedian, a main actor and chorus. The dancer performed the lavani, the comedian or the Songadya played with words and actions. The musical instruments were the 'Dholki' and the 'Tuntuna' somewhat like the dafli. Tamashas were popular during fairs and festivals and were greatly patronized during the time of Sawai Madhav Rao Peshwa and Baji Rao II. There are five divisions to the Tamasha. The Gan, an invocation to Lord Ganesha for blessings and success; The Gaulan, the dance of Lord Krishna and the 'gopis'; The Lavani where the dancer dances to the accompaniment of the love songs which are very suggestive; The Vag which is the enactment in prose and verse of a story of adventure and romance; and finally the Mujra where the dancer is a close parallel to the 'saki,' an influence that can be ascribed to the Moghul on local entertainment. Neela Bhalla observes: "what is also relevant is the overall tone, ambience and atmosphere of the play and the way in which he uses and adapts these features. The humour of the Songadya lay in his repartee and in his use of words with double entendre. This is a very integral part of Tendulkar's play." (134) For instance:

> Sutradhar: Ho! Ho! Ho! . . . Wait now, wait now. Hold your horses. Must you go?
>
> Brahman: Forces? Whose forces? Foreign? English? (362-63).

Or again

> Nana: Our grandeur's gone if she's not had.
>
> Servant: (bites his lips but acts with humility). Put your sword back in its sheath. Majesty. The prey is far away (380).

With the help of such dialogues, the playwright manages to keep a very fast and crisp pace, besides emphasizing the satiric tone. The mime adds to the brisk pace, doing away with elaborate stage properties and settings as in folk theatre as well as in European drama of the time. His Spartan style is reminiscent of modern western theatre. The music combines aspects of the Tamasha and the Dashavatar as well as the Bharud.

The chorus was used in ancient classical drama mainly to comment on moral values and positions and to fill in the time spans and action off the stage. Both Greek playwrights like Aeschylus and Sophocles and Roman dramatists like Seneca used the chorus. In Elizabethan drama, there was often a single character who spoke the prologue and epilogue. Sometimes as in *Antony and Cleopatra*, there was a choric character who also participated in the action. In Marathi folk drama, the role of the chorus was to serve the purpose of the refrain. It picked up and repeated the last few words spoken by the main character. It reminds us of the folk forms like 'Burrakatha,' and 'Oggukatha' of Andhra Pradesh in which we see the repetition of words. We see this kind of repetition in *Ghashiram Kotwal*, as in,

> Sutradhar: Reputation—must be preserved.
> Others: Be preserved.
> Sutradhar: Authority—must be preserved.
> Others: Be preserved. (406)

Ever since the first performance of *Ghashiram Kotwal* by the Progressive Dramatic Association of Poona, the play has successfully completed 1000 shows despite the controversy. When the play was invited to a drama festival in Berlin in 1979, criticism took a serious turn and eminent historians, actors, performers, artists and politicians all joined to protest against the play being staged overseas. It was only after the Oscar winner Satyajit Ray intervened and persuaded Mrs. Indira Gandhi to give her consent that the play was finally allowed to travel outside India. Vijay Tendulkar himself was quite unhappy about the controversy: "At times I feel that I should not have written *Ghashiram Kotwal*, as not only has it been the cause of personal turmoil, but it has also been the cause of many of my other plays being side-lined" (Naik 29).

However, in spite of all its controversies Tendulkar's *Ghashiram Kotwal* has remained a landmark in the history of modern Indian theatre.

II

The play *Ghashiram Kotwal* comprises only two acts. Act I of the play opens with the song in which Ganapati, Saraswati and Laxmi dance and Sri Gananaya is asked to bless the play. It deals with Ghashiram, a Brahmin from Kanauj, whose visit to Poona lands him in trouble as he is humiliated by the Poona Brahmins. He swears an oath of deep vengeance on the city of Poona. For this he offers his young and innocent daughter Lalita Gauri to Nana Phadnavis, the Peshwa's Chieftain and Magistrate of the city on whose weakness for women he thrives. In turn he demands that he be appointed the Kotwal of the city of Poona and becomes the in-charge of the law and order of Poona. He is at once on a spree of revenge perpetuating violence on his former tormentors. But it is sad to note that Ghashiram does not realize that Nana is merely using him as a weapon to keep the Brahmins of the city of Poona under check. When Ghashiram becomes the worst foe of the city Brahmins, Nana enjoys Gauri's innocent charms, makes her pregnant, kills her and gets her buried. The moment Ghashiram comes to know that Nana is marrying seventh time; he angrily confronts Nana who tells him that his innocent daughter's life is too small a price for him to get a significant post of Kotwal. At this time the city Brahmins unite with a strong demand for Ghashiram's death. Nana signs the death warrant as casually as he has signed the order of Kotwalship for Ghashiram. Finally we see Ghashiram being mobbed by the angry crowd of the city Brahmins who stone Ghashiram to death. When the city Brahmins gather round Ghashiram's dead body, Nana appears and declares the end of an age of terror and asks them to participate in the celebrations to mark the end of Ghashiram's Kotwalship.

Tendulkar's play goes back to a historical incident. Balaji Janardan Bhanu (1742-1800) was the Peshwa's Phadnavis of Poona. Being a shrewd statesman, he kept the British aggression with the help of his astute political strategy and statesmanship. He successfully reigned his political power till his death. He was a cult hero and people ignored his weakness of sex and womanization. They were blind to his treacherous designs. When he asked his people to stone their Kotwal to death, they never hesitated and followed his word as an order out of their blind faith and love towards him. It was this particular trait of character that Tendulkar sought to highlight in his play. According to Samik Bandyopadhyay: "in *Ghashiram* power is defined horizontally in terms of individuals against individuals, from humiliation to revenge in assertion, to eventual victimization; played out against a background of political and moral decadence and degeneracy, with sexuality impinging on strategies of power" (vii-viii).

Tendulkar's play is built in the backdrop of the city of Poona. The city of Poona is known for diverse things. It was known as cultural city. There was dominance of Brahmins right through ages. The city was the birthplace of Rashtriya Swayam Sevak Sangh (RSS), the premier religious wing of old Jana Sangh and the present Bharatiya Janata Party. Although it was dominated by Brahmins, there was a difference between the city Brahmins and the Brahmins belonging to other places in India. Despite their claim for superiority of race, they were notorious for treachery, greed and falsehood. To satiate their appetite, they would stoop to any level of debasement. To gain an upper hand they would exploit any situation to their favour. Tendulkar wonderfully shows this fact when Ghashiram confronts Nana for the first time. Nana lays his ankle on the back of Ghashiram while dancing with Gulabi. Ghashiram exploits this situation allowing Nana to rest his injured leg on his back. The resourcefulness of Ghashiram fetches him both the favour of Nana and anger of the city Brahmins who see in him a severe threat to their existence. So they make his life miserable and try to banish him from their society. In fact the Brahmins feel a sense of insecurity as much as Ghashiram.

Tendulkar admirably depicts the pathetic condition of the Brahmins in the *Dakshina* ceremony scene. Nana makes a mockery of this sacred ceremony by using it as a device to achieve his selfish ends. He feels happy and derives a sadistic pleasure when the Brahmins in their greed and anxiety grab the gifts that Nana throws at them. As Ghashiram joins them for the gifts, they beat him and throw him out. They hand him over to the soldiers accusing him of the theft of a purse. Despite his innocence, he is mercilessly and severely punished. His humiliation at the hands of the city Brahmins rouses his conscience against injustice and inhumanity. As he is strongly motivated by an intensely spiteful desire, he swears to teach them a lesson.

Ghashiram realizes that Nana is a womanizer who can do anything for the company of a woman. As a result, he works out a plan to please Nana by luring him through the charms of his innocent young daughter in order to secure a position of power and authority, Kotwal of the city of Poona. He declares in rage: "I'll come back to Poona; I'll show my strength. It will cost you! Your good days are gone. . . . You've made me an animal! I'll be a devil inside. I'll make Poona a kingdom of pigs" (376-77). There is an undercurrent of irony Tendulkar presents through the character of Ghashiram who represents an indiscriminate opportunism which ultimately becomes the cause of his downfall.

The character of Ghashiram is drawn from the historical character of Ghashiram Savaldas who belonged to the late eighteenth century Peshwa's Empire. Tendulkar's success as a playwright largely rests on his artistic ability by making this central character represent all phases of human history so as to fulfill the important trait of social realism. Smita Mishra comments on the character of Ghashiram: "His rise and growth from a Savaldas to the most controversial Kotwal of Poona is symbolic of the multifaceted growth of corruption in our society. Through the shrewd and opportunistic character of Ghashiram, Tendulkar has tried to bring out the truth that sycophancy not only flourishes but also prospers under the patronage of the rulers" (62).

Nana is strongly obsessed with the beauty of Ghashiram's daughter. He sees her at a religious ceremony where he follows her. Ironically when the girl is chased by him, she points to an idol and warns him "He will see." Then Nana tells her mockingly, "The idol of holiness? The maker of good? Look, he has two wives, one on this side, and one on that side. If you sit on our lap he won't say anything" (378). It is this utter disregard for the established institutions that Tendulkar excellently portrays in the play as a symbolic degradation of human values of modern society. Generally, the idol is a substitute for an invisible god. Human beings worship it with awe and fear. It keeps men on the path of upright behaviour. But out of greed when man becomes god himself, the practice of idol worship loses all its significance. On the other hand, it becomes a convenient device in the hands of people like Nana to perpetuate exploitation. As a result Nana who is a slave to passions transforms Poona into a hot bed of the pleasure-seekers. It is against this life of immorality that Ghashiram fights a war and becomes a martyr in the process at the end.

Sensing Nana's weakness for his daughter Gauri, Ghashiram gives his daughter away to Nana with a sense of satisfaction in trapping Nana through sex in order to achieve his goal. However, for a moment he is torn asunder by an inner conflict between an individual motivated by a sense of revenge and a responsible father. His conscience, therefore, pricks as he cries out:

> Oh, my daughter . . . the beast. . . . (Then yells at the audience) Oh, you people, look! I've given my beloved daughter into the jaws of that Wolf! Look! Look at this father. Putting the child of his heart up for sale. Look at my innocent daughter—a whore. That old overripe bastard! Look at him, eating her like a peach. . . . Spit on me. Stone me. Look, look, but I will not quit. I'll make this Poona a kingdom of pigs (381).

Ironically, Ghashiram sins more than sinned. He wants to drive sin out of Poona, but he commits himself a terrible sin by prostituting his own daughter. In this particular context, Smita Mishra pertinently observes: "Although Ghashiram, prompted by a desire to chastise his tormentors, surrenders his heart's child to Nana the devil, for mere Kotwalship, he is fully aware of his sin and wishes to save Gauri once he is declared Kotwal of Poona" (62).

The irony lies in Ghashiram's failure to understand the realistic situation in which he moves. He miserably fails to understand the inner designs of Nana and unknowingly gets into the trap laid by Nana. Ghashiram feels that he has succeeded in his clever plan, but tragically, he does not foresee the future trap into which he is entering. Nana has double advantage in appointing Ghashiram as the Kotwal: one sexual and two, political. He can enjoy his daughter as well as use him to control the Brahmins of Poona. In this connection Nana's words manifest his mindset:

> Go Ghashya, old bastard. We made you Kotwal. Raise hell if you wish. But you don't know the ways of this Nana. This time, there are two bullets in this gun. With the first one we'll fell your daughter. But with the second one we'll make the city of Poona dance, Ghashya, child, you are a foreigner. I've put you on Poona's back—why? As a counter check to all those conspirators, you'll not be able to join them; they'll never trust you even if you do because you are a stranger; an outsider. We just raised a dog at our door to the position of the Kotwal. We are your sole support. Oh! You are a bastard, Ghashya. . . . Our misdeeds will be credited to your account. We do it; our Kotwal pays for it. This opportunity comes in the shape of Ghashiram. And that luscious peach is at hand to be devoured by Nana. Excellent! Yes, Ghashya, be Kotwal. This Nana blesses you. (384-85)

Ghashiram takes over the charge of Kotwalship of Poona. He enforces the laws strictly. He declares that the delinquents shall be punished severely. Resultantly there is a considerable fall in the crime rate. The Brahmins of the city of Poona are frightened at the mention of his name. He asserts that nothing can be done without his knowledge. Permits should be obtained "to kill a pig, to do an abortion, to be a pimp, to commit a misdemeanor, to steal, to live with one's divorced wife, to remarry, to commit suicide" (387).

Ghashiram who is blinded by success with his Kotwalship becomes a demon. He misuses his power. For few days the city of Poona gets rid of its vulgarity under the strict vigilance of Ghashiram's Kotwalship, but there is a rise in evil activities too. The result of absolute power on Ghashiram is that it makes him ruthless, sadist and high handed in his treatment of the people who have hurt his feelings earlier. He uses savage methods to extract truth from culprits. His Kotwalship serves as a means to bring about a radical change in the city of Poona, but soon he becomes impatient and fails to understand the real causes for the crimes of the people. So within no time he becomes unpopular.

Though Ghashiram appears to be carried away by absolute power, he is aware of his responsibility as a father who thinks, "it is easy to find a bridegroom when one has money, jewels and respect!" (398). But he is shocked beyond measure when he comes to know about the death of his beloved daughter. He at once rushes to Nana to know the reason of his daughter's death. Nana who is as cunning as a fox pacifies him through his words and offering of his power.

The power with which Ghashiram wants to increase the happiness of his daughter is ruthlessly employed on the Brahmins of the city of Poona. As they are unable to bear the atrocities inflicted upon them by Ghashiram, they rise in revolt against him. They go to Nana and plead with him to end the rule of Ghashiram Kotwal. Nana who has been waiting for a chance "how to use a thorn to remove a thorn" encourages them to finish Ghashiram. The play ends with Ghashiram being stoned to death. In this context Smita Mishra's observation is significant:

> Ghashiram in his quest for power confronts Nana and plays his game to become the Kotwal of Poona foolishly thinking that the Kotwali will mean power in his hands, but Nana knows "what will happen is that our misdeeds will be credited to your account." As such Ghashiram is outwitted at the game of power played by Nana who exploits him as long as he needs him and drops him brutally in the end. Ghashiram's transformation from a poor and helpless Brahmin to a high handed Kotwal is a journey from the world of innocence to the world of experience (62).

The ultimate punishment given to Ghashiram is a substantial proof of the truth, "whoever violates the universal order gets violated by it." This law of retribution is expressed in the words of Nana:

> Ladies and Gentlemen. Citizens of Poona. A threat to the great city of Poona has been ended today (the crowd cheers). A disease has been controlled. The demon Ghashiram Kotwal who plagued all of us has met his death. Everything has happened according to the wishes of gods. (415)

Ghashiram's punishment is greater than what he actually deserves and so it rouses our pity and sympathy. Tendulkar successfully presents a striking character of a tragic hero in Ghashiram. Though the play is full of violence and torture, it is not shown physically so much as it is shown through physical gestures of the chorus and through the words of the Sutradhar. The violence that we see in the play exemplifies Tendulkar's awareness of the violence in the psyche of modern man.

Tendulkar's social realism in the play can also be seen in the portrayal of the helpless and hapless condition of women. He points out how Indian women are suppressed in a male-dominated society through the sacred institution of marriage and shows how vulnerable Indian women are in our patriarchal society. Ghashiram, the eponymous father, does not hesitate in bargaining the chastity of his daughter for his own selfish desire to avenge his humiliation on the people of Poona. For Nana Phadnavis woman is an object of sexual gratification only. Nana procures Gauri by making Ghashiram the Kotwal of Poona and for some time, as is reported by the Sutradhar; "Gauri orders, Nana does, Ghashiram's reign is here" (386). Nana however, has such an endless lust for women that he always needs a beautiful girl and new bride for the gratification of his sexual urges. Gauri's physical charms cannot satisfy him for long and it is soon reported that Nana is marrying a girl of fourteen.

Marriage is considered to be the holiest of holy institutions in our society. But Nana has a different way of looking at the sanctity of marriage. In spite of having several wives he's still going to marry a small girl. The Sutradhar reports:

> Let's go to the wedding.
> The Peshwa's Chief Minister.

> Still young enough to marry!
> His moustache's turned grey.
> He's got six wives.
> Look—that's not enough!
> So he's got a new one. (401)

Woman has no choice of her own in a male-dominated society and the situation is the same whether she is Gulabi or Gauri or the newly-wed wife of Nana or the old wives of Nana. Woman has always been a slave to her male counterpart, be it the eighteenth century or the twenty-first century. How the inner roots of social realism are projected in Tendulkar's play can be clearly seen through the playwright's effective handling of female sexuality to represent the loss and destruction caused by the struggle for power.

The corruption that power brings about is projected through the sexual laxity of the Brahmin dominated society of Poona. The play was attacked by those who perceived the play as an attack on the character of Nana Phadnavis, the finest administrator and one of the greatest patriots of the Maratha Empire. Tendulkar responded to this criticism by pointing out that Ghashiram Kotwal was not meant to be historically accurate account of Nana or Ghashiram's character. The most important thing is that he has examined the very modern issue of the relationship between power and gender in a patriarchal society in a historical setting with historically recognizable characters. By locating the story in the past and by associating it with a much admired and revered national figure, Tendulkar has underlined both the dark ambiguity of the cardboard figures of power which the male dominated society holds in high esteem and the dangers of this struggle for power in which gender has always played an important part. Meaning of gender in patriarchy is not just a "difference" but "division, oppression, inequity and inferiority for women" and thus for all those without access to power. Tendulkar in *Ghashiram Kotwal* suggests that the social construction of gender is effectively a useful tool in the hands of the powerful and lead inevitably to the dehumanizing of both the powerful and the powerless alike, the Nanas and the Ghashirams as much as the Gauris, and also to the destruction of meaningful human relationships and social and moral values.

Tendulkar's play assumes the dimension of powerful political satire in as much as it clearly presents the dark side of the ruling class of Maharashtra in all its facets. *Ghashiram Kotwal* is an attack on the moral downfall of the ruling class of Maharashtra who considered themselves custodians of public morality. It comments acerbically on political institutions of present day India where scores of Ghashirams are made and marred each time the political die is cast anew. The impulse to write the play was provoked by the contemporary political situation of the time, specifically the rise of power of the Shiva Sena in Maharashtra.

As part of his portrayal of social realism, Tendulkar in his play in Act One presents a wider cross-section of social stream of the city of Poona. The speaker of the play, Sutradhar, announces: "These are all Brahmins of Poona who are you?" (362) when he sees scores of people that appear in Poona.

The city of Poona attracts people from other parts of the country in view of its geographical, social and economic importance. When Sutradhar asks them, they introduce themselves:

> Oneman: A Vedantic Scholar.
> Sutradhar: You?
> Second: A Vaidya Doctor.
> Third: A Logician.
> Fourth: An Astrologer.
> Fifth: A Linguist.
> Sixth: I am a baron.
> Others: I come from Shingeri.
> I come from Tanjore.
> I come from Rameshwar.
> I come from Banaras.
> We're Poona people. (362)

This situation clearly shows how Poona has attracted people of other places of India into its social stream. The projection of social realism in Act One of the play is clearly manifested through the places apart from characters and situations. The Brahmins of the city of Poona always visit three important places namely Bavannakhani, the Temple, and the Graveyard.

Bavannakhani is the place where lives Gulabi, the courtesan, whom Nana regularly visits for sensuous pleasures. It has a great deal of dramatic significance because it is treated like Mathura. Here the Brahmin curtain is transformed into a group sitting in Gulabi's hall. A dancer dances. The dance is erotic. Ghashiram dances with her. He is her foil, sycophant ludicrous. All are involved in the erotic mood, attentive to her while they are equally attentive to him.

Brahmans often say that it is like Mathura, Bavannakhani. After the dance they whistle and throw turbans in the air. Then they demand the Brahman and Brahman wife to dance. Gulabi and Ghashiram bow, go to one side and reappear as Brahman and Brahman wife. The Brahman has a big stomach and his wife has long tuft of hair. They sing lavani and dance.

The Brahmans have lost themselves in Bavannakhani while their women are languishing at home without the fulfillment of their physical desires. In this context, Sutradhar the chief spokesperson of the play comments: "The Brahmans have lost themselves in Bavannakhani and the Brahman women are at home; they stay at home; oh yes, they stay at home. The Brahmans have lost themselves in the cemetery, in Kirtan; the Brahman women are sentenced to solitary confinement" (368).

The mention of the other two places; the cemetery and the temple is made by Sutradhar again in order to emphasize the association of the city Brahmins with these two places every day in one way or the other. We can see how realistically Tendulkar presents it through the words of Sutradhar:

> Night comes
> Poona Brahmans go

To Bavannakhani.
They go
To Bavannakhani.
They go to the cemetery
They go to the Kirtan
They go to the temple—as they have done every day.
The Brahmans go to Bavannakhani. (366)

There is yet another fact of social realism that Tendulkar presents in Act One of the play i.e., the crisis of the individual identity. When Ghashiram stands in the line along with other Brahmans of the city of Poona, soldiers accost him:

First Soldier:	Hey who are you?
Ghashiram:	Ghashiram Savaldas from Kanauj.
Second Soldier:	Go on. Move aside. Why are you here?
Ghashiram:	They are honouring Brahmans. There's a feast.
First Soldier:	What does that have to do with you?
Ghashiram:	I'm a Brahman too.
Second Soldier:	You a Brahman! Where is your shaven head? Where is your holy thread? Where is your pious look?
First Soldier:	Where is your holy book? Recite the hierarchy of caste. Tell us when did you last fast?
Second Soldier:	Looks like a thief?
First Soldier:	Looks like a scoundrel!
Ghashiram:	No, I'm a Brahman from Kanauj. New to Poona (373)

Tendulkar achieves dramatic unity in the play through Chorus and Sutradhar, the two important characters. Both sing a song of ecstasy at nights on several occasions suggesting that the urge for sexuality is presented through these songs.

Ram Shiva Hari
Mukunda Murari
Radha Krishna Hari
The streets of Bavanna become for a while the garden of Krishna.
Bavannakhani is like Mathura.

> Mathura avatarli!
> Ho, Bavannakhani! (367)

At this time Nana holding silver handled walking stick, garland of flowers on wrist appears. Dancer comes dancing, coming from back of line. Both dance. Ghashiram stands to one side in Brahman dress then:

> All Together: Radha Krishna Hari
> Govinda Murali
> Rama Shiva Hari
> Mukunda Murari (369)

These songs contain key words like Radha, Krishna, Hari, Govinda, Murali, Rama, Shiva, Hari, Mukunda, and Murari, suggestive of sexuality of the Brahmans and Nana through the grab of song and dance singing these songs every night.

When Nana chases Gauri, the innocent girl, through the garden, the Brahmans form a garden:

> The garden of Hira
> The garden of Saras
> The garden of Moti
> The garden of Poona
> Became the garden of Mathura where Krishna played. (381)

Tendulkar, on a realistic plane, projects the character of Nana as to symbolize the place where Nana hunts girls for fulfilling his physical gratification. Here it is interesting to note that the playwright intends to highlight how the people lionize the character of Nana in order to cancel his faults.

In Act Two of the play, the playwright presents a total transformation in the character and personality of Ghashiram. He rises from being a meek Brahmin to the position of Kotwal of Poona. In this context Sutradhar comments: "Gauri orders. Nana does, Ghashiram's reign is here. . . . Gauri dances, Nana dances, Ghashiram's got his chances" (386). Ghashiram displays his power and authority. He starts his rule by making the rounds of the city of Poona at night. Here Sutradhar rightly comments:

"Ghashiram Kotwal started making the rounds of Poona at night after eleven o'clock cannon. Started ruling in person. Accosted anyone he met in the streets. Whipped people. Arrested people. Demanded people's permits. Imprisoned people. Sued people." (387)

The prisons started filling. At night all the people have to stay at home: 'They have to stay with the wives they married.' The wives have to sleep with the men they are married to. They are compelled to be moral, not to abort to be wholesome, to stay alive. On new Kotwal's rule Sutradhar comments: "Prostitutes' lane was desolate. The chasing of women was halted. Pimps turned into beggars' counterfeit coins were worthless. Without a permit nothing can be done." (388)

Tendulkar in Act Two of the play drives home how the Brahmans of the city of Poona were subjected to physical violence, humiliation through his methods of oppression with an attitude of vengeance towards those Brahmans who insulted; humiliated and foisted falsely in theft. We can see it when Ghashiram orders a soldier to go to a Brahman's house to find out the truth. Whenever Ghashiram orders his soldiers, he twists his moustache so as to show his power and arrogance: "Go with him. Go to his house and make sure. If he's lying, take off his shirt and give him twenty five lashes. If he's a thief, an adulterer, a whore-monger, then tie up his hands and feet and throw him in a cell." (389)

Ghashiram declares that he will straighten out the adulterous city of Poona in six months. To a large extent he succeeds. But soon he faces the wrath of people as well as the intrigues of Nana resulting in his ultimate doom.

The quick sequence of the severe humiliations in addition to his hunger and poverty makes Ghashiram furious and enrages him to take revenge. Gulabi snatches his necklace and sends him out with the help of thugs. He loses both his employment and the necklace. He is severely beaten and imprisoned by soldiers on the charge of stealing money. All the Brahmins, Brahmin women, Gulabi, the Marathi lovers and others look down upon Ghashiram who feels immensely hurt at the insult he was put to and damage to his reputation for no fault of his. In retaliation, he says:

> But I'll come back. I'll come back to Poona. I'll show my strength. It'll cost you! Your good days are gone! I am a Kanauj Brahmin, but I've become a Shudra, a criminal, a useless animal. There is no one to stop me now, to mock me, to make me bend, to cheat me. Now I am a devil. You have made me an animal; I'll be a devil inside. I'll come back like a boar and I'll stay as a devil. I'll make pigs of all of you. I'll make this Poona a kingdom of pigs. Then I'll be Ghashiram again, the son of Savaldas once more. (376-77)

The urge for power, which is the only way to take revenge, forces Ghashiram to sacrifice his only daughter. He sends his daughter Gowri to Nana. Ghashiram, on the one hand, feels guilty about sacrificing his daughter and, on the other hand, feels urged to avenge the immense humiliation of the people of Poona. He cries out aloud and says:

> Now he's in my hands. . . . Oh, my daughter . . . the beast. . . . (Then yells at the audience) Oh, you people. Look! I've given my beloved daughter into the jaws of that wolf! Look! Look at this father. Putting the child of his heart up for sale. Look at my innocent daughter—a whore. That old overripe bastard! Look at him, eating her like a peach. . . . Spit on me. Stone me. Look, look, but I will not quit. I'll make this Poona a kingdom of pigs. (381)

Since Nana can't help enjoying sex with his daughter, Ghashiram blackmails him on this and urges him to make him the Kotwal of Poona. Nana issues the order making Ghashiram the Kotwal of Poona. Samik Bandyopadhyay in his 'Introduction' comments: "Tendulkar suggests the sexuality implicit in power in the brilliant innuendo that caps the situation" (iv).

Vijay Tendulkar has fully succeeded in depicting how Nana uses religion to enjoy both his sexual and political life. A whole aura of hymns and religious ceremonies provide the ironic scene that is pierced through by the crudest exercises of power. A typical example is the one in which Nana tries to seduce the girl praying before Ganapati, at the end of one of the ceremonies, and when the girl points to the god, saying 'He will see' (378), he says mockingly, 'That Idol of holiness?' (378) and the façade of ceremony collapses at once. Religion manifest in caste dominance and ceremony is a device of power in Ghashiram, but more as an abstraction of awe than as material force.

Another typical scene is the one in which Nana consoles Ghashiram, who loses his daughter. Nana quotes from the scriptures and advises him to forget the past: "The Vedas have said that. After all, Ghashya, will we live for ever? [Sighs] we too, every one of us, will leave Ghashya. . . . This body is earth, just dirt. You cannot rely upon it. What comes, that goes. Four handfuls of ash remain" (405). It is one kind of hegemonic attempt to oppress people in the name of religion. In addition to religious and sexual ceremonies, the deceptions of deputation constitute yet another device of power. Ghashiram starts persecuting the people who have humiliated him before and who also happened to be the enemies of Nana. Nana is happy that Ghashiram is doing what he himself wants to do. He makes Ghashiram a pawn in his power game. He says to himself:

> Go, Ghashya, old bastard. We made you. We made you Kotwal. Raise hell if you wish. But you don't know the ways of this Nana. This time, there are two bullets in this gun. With the first one we'll fell your luscious daughter. But with the second we'll make the city of Poona dance (384).

Even as Ghashiram, the fool that he is, thinks that the Kotwali will be power in his hands but Nana knows: 'What'll happen is that our misdeeds will be credited to your account.' Earlier Tendulkar has shown religiosity and sexuality combining in the strategies of power. Now he shows sexuality and the strategy of deputation working hand in hand. Once again, in Nana's words: "Bastard, you've got me in a narrow pass" Ghashiram answers: "Yes, the narrow pass of my only daughter." (384)

Samik Bandyopadhyay explains how Nana exercises his power safely through Ghashiram and how this reflects the contemporary political scene in India:

> Like ceremony, both religious and secular, the deceptions of deputation constitute yet another device of power. The real power uses the masks of deputation to mediate the exercise of power to hide from the victims the real face of power so that all resistance is effectively deflected. Intermediate democratic institutions, are the paraphernalia of bureaucracy, too often regarded as repositories of at least executive, are more often than not masks or mediations that veil the actual exercise of power and hide the perpetration from the eyes of the victim. (vi)

Tendulkar brilliantly comments on the pangs of the faithful wives whose unfaithful husbands "spend their treasure on foreign thighs." The wives of the whore-mongers wait faithfully for their men, but men are totally indifferent to their wives' physical and emotional needs. The Sutradhar rightly comments on the psychologically disturbed wives who are victimized by the institution of prostitution:

> The Brahmans have lost themselves in Bavannakhani and the Brahmin women are at home; they stay at home; oh yes, they stay at home. The Brahmans have lost themselves in the cemetery, in *Kirtan*; the Brahman women are sentenced to solitary confinement. (368)

It is an acknowledged fact that the prostitution is the oldest profession in the world, and politics and prostitution are not two different words with different meanings, but they are actually synonyms. A report prepared by the Advisory Committee of the League of Nations supports this view: "Prostitution has outlived every social, economic, ethical, and political system which the West has known since the time of the Greek states. It has had its vicissitudes; but flourishing or languishing, public or clandestine, it has existed in large towns for the last 2500 years, thereby proving how deeply it is rooted in human social life." (League of Nations Report 8)

Ghashiram Kotwal is not only a criticism of the institution of prostitution which nurtures the social evils like adultery and womanizing, but the play's significance and force tie in the playwright's indirectly conveyed message that the institution of marriage must be saved for the survival of social stability and harmony. Tendulkar perceives the realities of the human society without any preconceived notions, reacts to them as a sensitive and sensible human being and writes about them in his plays as a responsible writer.

The treatment of women characters in this play reflects the contemporary sociological condition. The two major women characters in this play are Gulabi and Gowri. Gulabi is a courtesan who encourages the sexual impulse in the public for her livelihood. The other character, Gowri is also used as a tool in the power game. The other minor characters like Nana's wives and a Brahmin lady also appear on the dais only in the situation of gratifying the sexual urge. Nana's wives appear only to dance with their husband when he is erotically engaged with other new girls. Gowri lacks the spirit to rebel against her father. It projects the male chauvinism which has been prevalent in the society till today. A young girl becomes an easy prey to the patriarchy in the form of her father's ambition. The audience or readers understand Gouri's passive submission to the old lechery in a sympathetic way which is nothing but the social reality. It shows the playwright's attempt to expose the mechanisms of patriarchy in the contemporary society.

Though the play was written in the early 1970s and the preceding decade was a period of great feminist activity, Tendulkar's purposeful denying of Gowri's voice in the play has at least two choices. Gowri neither shares her experiences of shame and humiliation nor protests and rages against being used as a commodity. Her natural dreams of love and fulfillment are shattered when at a very tender age she is made Nana's mistress. It is again through Ghashiram's agony only that the audience comes to know about the death of Gowri. The play exposes a patriarchal culture which traps women into destinies not of their choosing and legitimizes the violence against them.

Ghashiram's wife, though invisible on the stage, but referred to in the play, keeps silent on the offering of her daughter by her husband for illegal sexual contact with Nana without marriage. This shows the place of a woman in society. Even the wives of Nana never question him when he is engaged sexually with small young girls. Tendulkar's comment on the Indian mentality and the reality that lies beneath their attitude reminds us of history repeating itself. Tendulkar shows how Indians' national pride, unity and integrity are supplanted by self-interest and narrow religious and regional politics. The power struggle is an on-going process around India at national level as well as regional level. Talking about the playwright's timely and timeless message of the play how the infighting between the Moghuls and the Indians and the Indian rulers themselves led to an easy entry for British establishment Girish Karnad comments: "A decade after the play was written, in Punjab Sant Bhindranwale and Mrs. Gandhi seemed to be re-enacting the theme in real life in horrific death" (15). According to Girish Karnad Indian Folk Theatre has energy to uphold the traditional values and to question the present values. It can preserve both formative and thematic values. Interestingly, Tendulkar has applied these formative values to the themes and made the play fully applicable to the contemporary society which mirrors social realism. In fact, no other major playwright prior to Tendulkar has made such an extensive and innovative use of the folk theatre.

By now, the play has been performed more than 1000 times not only in various parts of India but also in several foreign countries such as France, the Federal Republic of Germany, the U.K., the Netherlands, etc. Moreover, with the play being prescribed in syllabus for not only the course in Marathi literature but also in the syllabus for English Honours students (in translation) of the University of Delhi, speaks volumes for the authenticity of the play both in theme and structure. It got rave reviews in *London Times*, *Guardian*, *Der Spiegel* and *NTQ*.

In spite of the flaws and attacks, the play can be considered Tendulkar's masterpiece, blending themes and forms and ends by suggesting some resultant ideas for discussion. The audience leaves the theatre with the consciousness that Ghashiram is dead only as a person but not as a system.

Works Cited

Bandyopadhyay, Samik. Introduction. *Collected Plays in Translation* by Vijay Tendulkar. Kolkata: Seagull, 1999.

Bhalla, Neela. "Ghashiram Kotwal: Text and Sub-text." *Vijay Tendulkar's Plays: An Anthology of Recent Criticism*, ed. V.M. Madge. Delhi: Pencraft International, 2009.

Bhalla, M.M. "Folk Theatre and Operas." *A Handful of Dreams*. Delhi: Kantas, 1977.

Juneja, Renu. "Two Modern Dramatists in Search of Tradition." *South Asian Review*, Vol. I. (Dec. 1980): 41.

Karnad, Girish. "Author's Introduction." *Nagamandala, Tughlaq, Hayavadana*. Delhi: Oxford University Press, 1994.

Mishra, Smita. "*Ghashiram Kotwal* as a Political Play." *Contemporary Indian Dramatists*, ed. Shubha Tiwari. New Delhi: Atlantic, 2007.

Noble Dass, Veena. *Modern Indian Drama in English Translation,* Hyderabad: Taurus, 1988.

Naik. "Ghashiram Kotwal Remains Controversial." *The Times of India* June 20, 2000: 11.

"Prevention of Prostitution." *League of Nations Report*. Geneva: 1943.

Sakharam Sardesi, Govind. *New History of the Marathas*. Vol. IV. Bombay: Phoenix, 1948.

The 1960s and 1970s witnessed a lot of feminist activity. Mary Wollstonecraft's *A Vindication of the Rights of Women* (1792), J.S. Mill's *The Subjection of Women* (1869) and Simone de Beauvoir's *The Second Sex* (1949) were precursors of this movement. Kate Millett's *Sexual Politics* in 1969 was a landmark.

Kamala: Phallocentrism and Sensational Journalism

Tendulkar's play *Kamala* is based on a real life incident reported in *The Indian Express* by Ashwin Sarin, a journalist, who really bought a woman in a rural flesh market and presented her at a press conference to expose the inhuman flesh trade. Taking this incident as his theme, Tendulkar has modified it to suit his play. This attests what Tendulkar has said, "I have written about my own experiences about what I have seen in the others around me" (71). Though the play *Kamala* was first staged in the year 1981 by Kalarang in the direction of Kamalakar Sarang, it was published in the year 1982 and was translated into English by Priya Adarkar.

Tendulkar actually started his career as a journalist. As part of his profession, he moved around and observed the society closely. Later he started writing editorials with the information received from the second hand sources. But he was not satisfied with that. The dissatisfaction he has grown with has aroused his sense of conscience as a human being. It has made him restless. He says: "It started with my journalistic dissatisfaction, but it grew into much bigger proportions in the sense that it became a matter of conscience as a human being. I became restless" (5). The social maladies like the violence and the exploitation and the differences in the society that he witnessed made him restless. Though journalism could not offer him a solution for his mental disturbance, it helped him mould his dramatic career. Gowri Ramnarayan aptly points out: "With his exposure to Marathi theatre from childhood and journalistic background, Vijay

Tendulkar turned contemporary socio-political situations into explosive drama" (13).

Tendulkar's *Kamala,* certainly, is a powerful exposure against sensational journalism, where reporting can be affected not only by the personal attitudes but also by the selfish motives of journalists. Now, Tendulkar arrives with the plight of a woman, a theme of his great interest which he has already presented through plays like *Silence! The Court is in Session, The Vultures* and *Sakharam Binder.* The play is not only about sensational journalism but also about its adventurous investigations made not for the sake of welfare of the society but for the sake of name and fame which explores women (human) trafficking in general and exposes gender discrimination in the matrix of patriarchy in particular. The play also discusses the prevailing success syndrome attitude among journalists. The play not only brings out the evils of sensational journalism which exposes the real scenario of women's exploitation but also brings out the hegemonic and sexist behaviour of educated and elite men like Jaisingh Jadav. An educated and self-assured Sarita realizes her position, when she is asked an innocent question by an illiterate, tribal woman Kamala, "How much did he [Jaisingh] buy you for?" (34) One can easily understand how close their respective positions in society are underneath the surface differences of class.

Tendulkar unearths the suffering of the Indian middle class women at the hands of selfish, malicious and hypocritical male chauvinists. The theme of man-woman relationship, to which he gives much significance in his plays, is expertly touched upon in the complex relationship between Jadhav and his wife Sarita. The play *Kamala* is a gyno-centric play in which Tendulkar conspicuously focuses on the self-revelation of Sarita emerging from being a docile wife to an asserted, determined woman with self-knowledge in the end.

Jaisingh Jadhav is a successful journalist, who works for an English newspaper and lives in Delhi. He is self-centred and a man of arrogant disposition, who considers women as objects to be used and thrown away. His wife Sarita is educated and intelligent. She is portrayed as a replica of a good, educated Indian housewife who can look after her home and husband's needs in a perfect manner. Kakasaheb, Sarita's uncle, who is a newspaper editor and journalist, represents the old generation who does not like the way of functioning of the modern journalism which craves for sensationalism, lacking ethics. As part of his sensational journalism Jaisingh purchases a village woman, Kamala, in some place of Bihar to show the world that flesh trade still exists in India. He wants to present Kamala at a press conference to prove that the allegation of police that press men lie is wrong. Through innocent and ignorant Kamala, Sarita realizes the real nature of her husband and her position at home. She comes to know that she is also a slave and bonded labourer like Kamala. Sarita decides to reveal the real side of the nature of her husband to the world by arranging a press conference. At this time only she knows that Jaisingh is sacked from his job. Jaisingh becomes a pawn in the political chess game played by his newspaper owner, for conducting press conference as there are big shots involved in the flesh trade. The play ends with Sarita's decision of giving moral support to her husband in his troubled times for the time being and continues to be compassionate human being. The play concludes on an optimistic note with Sarita's resolution that she will stop being a slave in future.

The facts of Sarin's story, however, were only a basis for Tendulkar's play. Basically, the play raises two important questions. Whether this form of journalism does not turn out to be equally exploitative with its intention to expose women traffic and does the position of illiterate, rustic women who are kept for auction in the bazaar have any difference from the position of educated, elite, independent thinking urban women in a patriarchal society. Tendulkar creates and moulds the characters and situations in *Kamala* accordingly to explore these issues. That is why the entire play is structured around three long conversations. The first is between Kamala and Sarita, the second between Jadhav and Sarita's uncle, an old-style journalist who is also a newspaper owner-editor, and the third between Sarita and her uncle. More importantly it is the discussion between Kamala and Sarita that is significant because in it only an educated Sarita is enlightened and knows her position. This change is witnessed by the audience/readers in the discussion between Sarita and her uncle. The discussion between Jaisingh and Kakasaheb about new journalism though appears to be merely academic exposes in a way the degeneration of values interspersed with hypocrisy and sensationalism in the present scenario of modern journalism. The focus on the importance of debating the issue mirrors Tendulkar's social realism.

Journalists are supposed to be concerned with the absolute 'truth.' With a sense of public accountability and social responsibility, a journalist must be honest in providing reports of honest information. It is like an intellectual war. Print media has a great role to play in a democratic system in reflecting the varied opinions on vital issues. Freedom of press reflects freedom of expression which is guaranteed by the constitution. Therefore, the newspapers have to enhance that freedom by making people think rationally and express the same freely because a free press and democracy are inseparable. In this context it is apt to quote here *London Times* (1852): "The first duty of the press is to obtain the earliest and most correct intelligence of the events of the time, and instantly, by disclosing them to make them the common property of the nation. The press lives by disclosures. . . . The duty of the journalist is the same as that of the historian—to seek out the truth, above all things, and to present to his readers not such things as statecraft would wish them to know but the truth near as he can attain it." (Heren 16)

Talking about the influence of Media, Tendulkar says at the time of receiving the Katha Chudamani Award, "Earlier, literature did have an influence on society. Today, it is media persons and politicians who wield considerable influence and together they can do anything" (54). Tendulkar's comment on politics and politicians has resulted in so much criticism against him, especially when he reacted against Gujarat genocide. Many theatre and media people believed that Tendulkar should not get mixed up with politics. But Ayachit Santosh, one of the acquaintances of Tendulkar, comments on the issue: "I totally disagree. I believe art and politics can never be separated. You can't separate art and politics because politics is life. It is also a fact that life is political and art is about life, so it is inevitable that art should be political."

In most of Tendulkar's plays, women play an important role. Most of them are projected as victims by highlighting their gender stereotyping, namely—Laxmi, Champa, Benare, Mrs. Kashikar, Jyoti and now Sarita. They should suppress and sacrifice their will and desires to the subjugation and subordination of the male-dominated society. Such cultural hegemony definitely stops her personality from flowering. Women's subjugation in a patriarchal order of society is real. The violence is real. And this reality which is reflected and projected by Tendulkar in his plays is poignant. According to Sonia, "Jaisingh's attempt to prove flesh-trade as an inhuman practice in Indian context, of course, with his pretentious imbibed commercialistic ideology, typically exemplifies "the cultural approach to the media" (77). The cultural approach looks at the media as an institution which operates within a given culture in relation to which reporters perform their duties. This approach argues that a ruling ideology is not imposed but appears to exist by virtue of an 'arrived at' consensus. In other words, hegemony works by way of discourse and not necessarily through political and economic power.

Though Tendulkar says, "I do not align myself to any political ideology" his interest and observation of the society and his own personal experiences of life force him to say: "I do have my sympathies with the Left" (111). Perhaps his sympathies towards Leftist Ideology must have made him think in a woman's perspective which is reflected in most of his plays. His Left bias can be clearly seen in some of his plays like *Ghashiram Kotwal* and *Encounter in Umbugland,* where tyranny is ultimately defeated.

Vikram Gokhale, a well-known actor in Marathi drama, cinema and T.V. serials, after doing one hundred and thirty shows of *Kamala* throughout the state of Maharashtra, raises some serious objections against Tendulkar's dramatic intentions in the play (152). He sees three reasons that give rise to these questions. 1. The entire character of Jaisingh Jadhav and his ideology: whether Jaisingh is supposed to be something else. 2. The character of Kakasaheb, and the gap between his words and deeds: whether he cynically mocks at Sarita's suffering by telling her that she has no alternative or whether he is trying to gloss over his own male chauvinism. It is not certain whether he really opposes Jaisingh. 3. The gap between the thoughts and ideas centring round Sarita, and the ending of the play: whether Tendulkar wants to suggest that Sarita, because she represents Indian wife, is a masochist, and if so does she remain so, because she has no other alternative. It is doubtful whether for Tendulkar a woman in a male-dominated society, no matter where she is, no matter of what religion or caste, no matter educated or uneducated is necessarily a Kamala or whether Kamala is a particular tendency. It is not clear whether she represents masochist tendency or whether she is a parody of some of the orthodox Indian notions of the wife's duties. According to Sudhir Sonalkar:

> Almost all the characters in *Kamala* are hastily drawn. It is almost as though Tendulkar saw dramatic potential in a newspaper story and wanted to pounce on it before anyone else did. But there is almost inexplicable element in the play. The journalist's wife detests the whole incident and says that the Kamala incident has taught her that she too is a slave. The connection is very weakly brought out. The play is shoddily and hurriedly written. But what is this about after all? . . . Nothing is developed. No character becomes a focal point and the play leaves you simply untouched. (21)

Yet, *Kamala* as a film succeeded in creating an impact on the Indian screen. Tendulkar once again succeeds in depicting the status of women in the present-day society in comparison to the male chauvinistic world of today.

II

The play contains two Acts. There are no scene divisions. The background is Neeti Bagh, a posh locality in the metropolitan city, Delhi. When the curtain rises, Kakasaheb, Jaisingh's wife Sarita's uncle, is seen speaking on the phone. Obviously the phone call is for Jaisingh who is out of station. Within no time we witness non-stop phone calls, which are received and noted by Sarita as if it is her primary objective. However, the dramatic purpose of the hectic phone calls contributes to the principal theme of the play. When Kakasaheb asks her why she wants the name of the caller to whom he has just been talking, Sarita replies: "I have to write down each phone call" (3). If she fails to do so, in Sarita's words, "If I say they did not tell me their names he [Jaisingh] gets angry with me for not asking" (3). These words of Sarita remind us of some old generation's grandmothers who make certain statements against their husbands which are mixed with some sort of pride. Sarita's sheer modesty which is prominently signified in these words looks to be awkward. As Sarita represents the educated, independent-thinking and sophisticated women, it seems education makes women still sophisticated slaves without their notice. Education must improve one's awareness and augment one's self-respect. Like Kamala, Sarita too becomes a mere pawn in Jaisingh's game of chess. Sarita is seen as a well-educated modern woman who takes care of her brilliant and agile husband in every aspect. Right from the taking telephonic messages and notes to keeping delicious food and intoxicating drinks for him, Sarita is a replica of modern educated housewife and a passionate woman who cares and loves her husband. This is another dimension of Tendulkar's portrayal of his women characters.

Jaisingh Jadhav is a reputed young journalist who is working for an English daily published by an amoral press baron, Sheth Singhania. He is self-centred and a man of arrogant disposition. Sarita is his wife. She is well-educated and hails from a village named Phalton. They live in a small bungalow in a posh locality around New Delhi in the neighbourhood of Neeti Bagh. Kamalabai is Sarita's servant-maid and she too hails from Phalton. Kakasaheb is Sarita's uncle and he is currently in Delhi in order to obtain his quota of news print with Jadhav's help. Born in an aristocratic family, Kakasaheb runs a newspaper in the vernacular. He believes in Gandhian principles and lives a simple life. Kakasaheb's every conversation with either Sarita or her husband Jaisingh typically brings out the contrast between the two kinds of journalism. When Kakasaheb criticizes the "High Speed type" journalism practised by Jaisingh and his craze for "Eye-witness report," Sarita defends her husband saying if the things like "murder, bloodshed, rape, atrocity and arson happen, doesn't he be there?" (6) Kakasaheb immediately reacts to Sarita's words:

> Why does he have to? My dear, it's not the facts of an occurrence that are important. But the topic is. Discuss that. Comment on it. Suggest a way to stop it—suggest that. After all, any murder, rape or arson is like any other. What difference can there be? What sort

> of journalism is it that smacks its lips as it writes blood-thirsty descriptions instead of commentary? Its business isn't news—it is bloodshed! (6)

The above words of Kakasaheb which are replete with wisdom and experience support the type of journalism in which topic is important, not sensationalism.

Kakasaheb feels honoured and ecstatic when Sarita tells him that his house boy, who turns to be a defence minister, now enquires after him whenever he meets Sarita and Jaisingh at a party in New Delhi. Kakasaheb's response, in this context, is tinted with bitter sarcasm and his words clearly signify that there is a 'world of difference' between his way of journalism and that of Jaisingh. He says:

> I'm honoured. Who asks after me now? I'm a back number—remnant of times past. A dead journalist—Who's just about staying alive! Now it is the day of your husband's type of journalism. The High-Speed type! . . . Eye-witness report! (5)

Then the discussion between Sarita and Kakasaheb takes place about the threatening calls they receive, by which Jaisingh is threatened to kill for his news item about an M.P. who locked up his servant and thrashed him illegally, suspecting theft.

At this time, Jaisingh arrives with Kamala, a tribal woman, whom he has purchased from some place in Bihar. Kakasaheb, somehow, does not like the way of Jaisingh's functioning which is involved with sensationalism and always a threat to his life—especially the manner of his reporting which angers the people in power. His craving for 'Eye-witness' (5) in collecting the information and saying 'being on the spot—that's what's important! Never mind what you write' (5) appear to be the strategies of trendy journalism practised by Jaisingh which is detested by Kakasaheb.

Tendulkar projects that conspiracies and bloodthirsty professional plots are part and parcel of modern journalism. In the conversation which takes place between Jaisingh and

Kakasaheb about the modern journalists and their ways of collecting the news, Kakasaheb's sarcasm is visible:

> everyday . . . some fresh mal-masala from every nook and corner of the district. . . . Everyday new movements, new exploitations, new intrigues, exposures and counter-exposures. Higher circulation, more advertising, more income. Respectability and a packet of money—instead of standing in the doorway waiting patiently for some thing good to happen. (23)

Kakasaheb says he is not like the employer of Jaisingh because he will not be able to manage two or three newspapers and a skyscraper in every big city. His appetite is small. If he could save enough in ten years or so, his family would never want money. These words of Kakasaheb disclose how modern journalism has become commercial. Tendulkar, through the character of Kakasaheb, highlights the other side of the journalism which strictly follows professional ethics.

Jaisingh purchases the tribal woman Kamala for two hundred and fifty rupees in the Luhardaga Bazaar in Bihar to prove that there still exists flesh trade in some parts of India. Noticing Sarita's reaction, he says: "They sell human beings at this Bazaar . . . they have an open auction for women of all sorts of ages" (14). He goes on saying: "The men who want to bid handle the women, inspect them. How they feel in the breast, in their waist, in their thighs and . . ." (14). In a state of resentment, Sarita asks him to stop. Tendulkar's heart-rending depiction of buying and selling women in the flesh market brings out another important aspect of the play. 'Even a bullock costs more than that' (14), shows his human perspective which is a unique quality of his writing. This inhuman practice of buying a woman as one buys a hat or an apple, as Vikram Gokhale rightly puts, is "a sort of concubinage permanently subjugating the female slaves to the will of the masters" (152). He uses Kamala merely as an object who will enhance his professional prospects. He does not allow her to take bath, to sleep and takes her to press conference against her will in a torn sari. Through this Tendulkar seems to tell that women traffic is occurring among the economically and culturally challenged people like Dalits and Adivasis.

Jaisingh warns Sarita strictly not to tell anyone that he is going to exhibit Kamala at the 'press conference' to prove that the government's allegation against newspaper men is wrong. He feels excited at the very thought of press conference and foresees: "There will be high drama at today's press conference. It will create an uproar!" (15). Kamala is so ignorant and illiterate that she does not even know in which city she is. The deceptive and misleading mentality is very clear when Jaisingh says to her that he is going to take her to a place where 'big feasts' take place and that the people there "will want to meet her" (20). Jaisingh's order with a harsh voice, "you will have to come Kamala," in spite of Kamala's unwillingness to go in her torn clothes, tells more about his inhuman nature of trendy journalism. Poor Kamala had no other go than to follow her master. When Jaisingh tells her she has to answer to questions she is asked Kamala's innocence is disclosed in asking: "Do I have to tell everything? How we starved? How we had no clothes" (21). This reflects the impoverished and heart-moving lives of Adivasis in India which depicts social realism. When Sarita asks for Jaisingh's permission of her giving a sari to Kamala, Jaisingh's reaction is outrageous. Sarita is dampened by his anger. Jaisingh's longing to show something sensational that was unprecedented in the world of journalism is seen in his words. "She will come to the press conference in the same clothes she is wearing now" (21). When asked being a woman how can she be presented in torn clothes, as usual Jaisingh's male dominance snubs Sarita: "I know! You don't have to tell me, understand? . . . I want her to look just as she is at the press conference. It's very important" (22). By seeing the real side of her husband, the layers on Sarita's eyes slowly and gradually start melting now.

Kakasaheb's persuasion of Jaisingh's presenting Kamala in the press conference is not fruitful as Jaisingh defends it as an act which is involved with a social commitment. But his chief and selfish motive in such an act is very clear. He is definitely doing it for his promotion and publicity. It is conspicuous he is not doing it for the cause of women or downtrodden. Basically he is a male-chauvinist and an egotist. He does not believe in women's power or potential. In his opinion they are secondary in every aspect. They have no heart and no mind and rather puppets in the hands of men which can be used according to their will and wish. Tendulkar's unbiased and uncompromised depiction of male chauvinism through the character of Jaisingh represents his social realism.

Kakasaheb, then, asks Jaisingh what he hopes to gain from the reports that he writes in English which will certainly not be read by the common man whose cause Jaisingh is fighting. Here, Tendulkar highlights the contrast between journalism in the vernacular alone that reaches the masses, which is totally ignored and neglected by Jaisingh and entrapped himself in the clutches of capitalism which he realizes later. However, he is under the illusion that he will be protected by both his editor and his boss, in the crisis. Jaisingh's endeavour in convincing Kakasaheb that neither it was a game nor he was involved in 'it' for the sake of the things Kakasaheb mentioned shows the harsh hypocrisies of yellow journalism.

Moreover, Jaisingh's saying that it is nothing but his commitment towards the downtrodden and there is a social purpose in it is irony of all ironies. He further tells that there is a great need today for somebody to do it. In the moral rot someone has to uphold moral principles, norms and values. Someone has got to hold back the uncontrolled licence of those who have the machinery of power in their hands. The weak and backward sections of society are under attack. We need someone to make a noise about it. These words of Jaisingh remind us of giants reciting sacred scriptures; they have great dramatic significance later in the play, as we are to witness the real form of his social commitment towards the weaker sections of society.

Kakasaheb says that mercenary journalism is not a bad one if one could manage it. Though there may be danger in it, there's profit also. He gives a living example of Jaisingh himself which exposes the hypocritical ways of trendy journalism:

> For example, five years ago you were living in the shed outside a house in Karol Bagh. And today you're in a bungalow in Neeti Bagh—even it is a small one. You have servants, you have a car. You travel by plane all over the country. You stay in five star hotels. You get invitations from foreign embassies. You have access to ministers and Chief Ministers—or even to the Prime Minister! What's bad about that? The moral is there's no harm in this game—if you know how to play it right. (23)

Presenting Kamala in the press conference is nothing but showing *tamasha* for the journalists like Jain. Kakasaheb calls it a drama and it seems, performing a drama or *tamasha* in the Press Club. With this sort of game, playing with the life of an innocent tribal woman Kamala not only exposes the cruel, hypocritical nature but also the ignorance and naiveté of journalists. The questions posed to Kamala by the journalists in the press conference expose the foolishness of the journalists. The questions were like the questions posed to a Minister. "What are the important social problems in your area? What are your opinions about the economic exploitation of the tribals?" and a question on 'above the poverty line and below the poverty line' show the ignorance and the immaturity of the journalists.

Moreover, when they pose a question on tribal women's free sex, their sexual laxity and hypocritical, sadistic nature is revealed. According to Jaisingh and Jain the press conference was not serious, in other words it was fun for them. It reminds us of Benare's exposing of personal life in the name of 'mock trial' by the judges in *Silence! The Court is in Session*, another play of Tendulkar. Though Benare is not ignorant and innocent like Kamala, the ruthless silence imposed on her in the game played by the men is also compared with the silence of Kamala in the Press Conference. Tendulkar's portrayal of unveiling the complexities of human nature is a prominent characteristic of his plays. In *Gidhade* it is the pack of human vultures pitched against a defenceless female character, Rama. In *Silence! The Court is in Session,* it is Miss Benare against a pack of middle class vultures. In *Kamala* it is again Kamala against a pack of so-called educated journalist vultures.

This kind of conducting 'press conference' by Jaisingh and his eagerness to throw the 'whole caboodle in the government's lap'—is a way of "social organization of news"—a prevalent feature of trendy journalism. When Sarita says about Kamala that "She's innocent poor thing" (13), Jaisingh replies: "She looks one right now. But these people can be very smart too. Give them half a chance" (13-14). This sarcastic and inhuman comment of Jaisingh signifies his hypocritical attitude towards the downtrodden.

A reporter's sources of gathering news and picking up stories are the locations like police stations, courts, hospitals, corporations, political chambers etc. Thus news is constructed within the parameters of a bureaucratic universe. Newspapers need bureaucracies because the journalistic system of account production is itself bureaucratically organized. Therefore, the press normally records what has been recorded for it by working of institutions. It obviously re-presents those events which take place outside the purview of reporters. Ordinary people have remote chance of being caught in the news net, since they lack power. But 'unknown' like protesters, victims, voters get into the media only when involved in unusual activities, natural disorders and calamities.

Sarita is shocked at the way Kamala has been treated at the 'press conference.' She asks: "So while they were asking her those terrible questions, and making fun of her—you just sat and watched, did you?" (30) This reaction shows that only women can understand the problems of women. In journalism too, women tend to be more interested in their readers, more concerned about the background and the context of stories, more enquiring about experiences than end results. In a personal interview Jaya Menon, a renowned journalist, says: "I personally tend to believe that a woman understands issues or events in a large context than a man. It may not be the most rational, intellectual thinking. There may be even a slight touch of emotion, but certainly it is a very human way of thinking. I think woman makes better analyst than man" (62).

An inebriated and annoyed Jaisingh tries to convince both Kakasaheb and Sarita of the 'social purpose' behind the 'press conference,' saying "I did not hold this press conference for my own benefit. It was to drag this criminal sale of human beings into the light of the day" (31). At this Kakasaheb says: "And you sold a woman to them to do so" (31). Thus, he drives home the fact that Jaisingh has been more 'inhuman' under the pretence of 'humanizing the news in media' (Christmas 213). Linda Christmas argues that her research on UK Women Journalists demonstrates: (i) Women journalists tend to put readers' needs above those of policy makers. (ii) Women are inclined to be more people-oriented rather than issue-oriented. (iii) Women emphasize news in context rather than in isolation. (iv) Women prefer to clarify the consequences of events.

Media persons' role cannot be denied when it comes to the 'women's question.' Most of the times, the news of atrocities on women are highlighted by way of sensationalizing. Generally their bulk coverage of the news contributes to cricket, film stars, pop music, fashion parades, astrology and so on. While there were 512 accredited journalists covering the Lakme India

Fashion Week, there were only six journalists to cover the suicides in Vidarbha. In that Fashion Week Programme, the models were displaying cotton garments while the men and women who grew the cotton were killing themselves an hour away from Nagpur in the Vidarbha region. Nobody told that story except one or two local journalists. (Katju, Markandey. "Ideal and Reality: Media's Role in India." *The Hindu*, Aug. 19, 2008) No doubt, sometimes the media mentions farmers' suicides in Maharashtra, the rise in the process of essential commodities, and so on. But such coverage at the most constitutes five to six per cent of the total coverage. Is this a responsible way for the media to function?

Jaisingh receives many compliments for his press conference and feels very happy. As the police are after him to take Kamala to 'Nari Niketan,' an orphanage, Sarita opposes this and requests him to allow Kamala to stay with them in their house. Then, the cruel male chauvinist in him wakes up and says: "It's I who take decisions in this house, and no one else" (42). He takes Kamala to the orphanage and attends a party in the evening. What Simon de Beauvoir says about the modern men applies aptly to Jaisingh here: "The men of today show a certain duplicity of attitude which is painfully lacerating to women; they are willing on the whole to accept woman as a fellow being, an equal, but they require her to remain the inessential" (291). Suddenly, Sarita realizes her place in the house. Now, knowing the real side of her husband, she tells Kakasaheb that she is going to convene a press conference at which she intends to declare before the whole world, the real state of affairs at home:

> I am going to present a man who in the year 1982 still keeps a slave, right here in Delhi, Jaisingh Jadhav. I am going to say this man's a great advocate of freedom. And he brings home a slave and exploits her . . . the other slave he got free—not just free—the slave's father shelled out the money—a bigsome. (46)

When a startled and incredulous Kakasaheb asks her, "What on earth happened between you two?" (46), Sarita replies 'Marriage' (46). Here, in one sense the play *Kamala* can be seen a butt of satire on the husband-wife relationship that has come under increasing threat in the present society. When Kakasaheb asks her why she suddenly begins to think strangely in this way, Sarita says:

> I was asleep, Kamala woke me up. With a shock, Kamala showed me everything. . . . I saw that the man I thought my partner was the master of a slave. . . . Slaves don't have rights. . . . Laugh, when he says, laugh. Cry, when he says, cry . . . when he says lie on the bed—they. . . [*She is twisted in pain.*] (46)

Tendulkar has, in a way, succeeded to reflect the life of Indian educated and elite women through the delineation of the character of Sarita.

Through the character of Jaisingh's colleague Jain, Tendulkar is able to depict the true nature of rat race that goes on in this milieu. As one proceeds through the play, there is a growing realization that relations within the professional community are far less supportive, generous and harmonious. Jain, Jaisingh's friend, now comes to inform Sarita and Kakasaheb the shocking news that Sheth Singhania, the unscrupulous press baron, who has changed his stand towards politicians, has dismissed Jaisingh—a result of Jaisingh's exposure of flesh trade at the press conference. Sarita, at once, asks Jaisingh over the phone to come back from the party. Jaisingh returns and asks Sarita why she has called him away from the party. Sarita replies in an ironical tone; "Your owner is pleased with you and he's decided to relieve you from your job" (49). Jaisingh is shocked to hear the news and he curses his boss and then goes on banging his fist on the table, bursting out: "The bastard! Do you hear me? He is a bastard. That Sheth Singhania! I will teach him a lesson" (50).

Tendulkar's satirical exposure of the power-hungry politicians who amass wealth and build skyscrapers in metropolitan centres like Delhi shows his reflection of social realism. Jaisingh is under the illusion that he will be protected by both his editor and his boss, in the event of any danger. But he turns to be a victim at the hands of his owner, in other words he was exploited by his owner as he has exploited Kamala for his selfish motives. Now, he himself becomes another Kamala in the play. Coming from the background of journalism, Tendulkar is fully aware of the problems that are involved in trendy journalism. But Tendulkar as a realist does not tend to portray Jaisingh as a modern hero of bringing out hidden things of the dark world of the politics as we witness in the commercial movies. Moreover, he shows Jaisingh as a kind of villain who mingles with politicians in order to carry out their evil plans against democratic order. Here, Tendulkar establishes a truth; united politicians and media people can do anything to Indian society.

Sarita's position in the play brings out how typical Indian women have been shaped, conditioned and marginalized by patriarchy. The play highlights the gender stereotyping that is forced upon them. The roles allotted to women in patriarchal set up are purely domestic—daughter, wife, sister and mother. As part of the cultural hegemony, right from her childhood, the girl is taught to believe in the importance of 'family values'—values which are considered to be her responsibility only and not the male's. Sarita's acceptance of her subordinate position in the house and Kakasaheb's encouraging the continuance of the status express in a subversive way the question whether it is an act of self-sacrifice or a mere product of social conditioning.

Economics plays a vital role in women's life in patriarchy. A woman who has economic independence will be able to fight the conflicts in her life. Tendulkar seems to convey this message through the character of princess Vijaya in *Encounter in*

Umbugland who can succeed in defeating the ways of patriarchy to a great extent. Even in *Silence! The Court is in Session,* Benare is able to fight the conflicts in her life because of her economic independence which gives her courage to defy the male-dominated society. In Tendulkar's plays, male characters find more place in sociology than psychology. A remark of Kakasaheb corroborates this idea. To Sarita's question why only women must suffer quietly while men are addressed for their so-called achievements, Kakasaheb answers: "You're wrong. Sarita, my girl, doesn't a man make mistakes? . . . If you put your hand in the ox's mouth, it's going to feel cold. . . . You'll feel cold whether you're a man or a woman" (47). As Vikram Gokhale points out, Kakasaheb's character is ambiguous to the audience/ readers. While convincing Sarita in this way, does he want to convey that as long as the system of marriage goes on, it will go on like this? But Sarita doesn't agree with Kakasaheb. She says firmly, "What a man does is manhood must be changed" (47).

Sarita's ironical cry is an indirect call for women to react against not only yellow journalism but also hypocritical men in patriarchy. Her views penetrate into the weak areas of a few women's voluntary submission which ultimately brings a stigma to the whole world of women.

It is true Kakasaheb makes some feeble attempts to convince Sarita, but all his efforts are of no use. For she screams at him:

> Why? Why can't men limp behind? Why aren't women ever the masters? Why can't a woman at least ask to live the same way as a man? Why must only a man have the right to be a man? Does have one extra sense? A woman can do everything a man can. (47)

Such kind of sudden illumination of Sarita makes the spectators or readers understand the agony and genuine cry of women to enjoy equal rights with men. She is in no way inferior to a man in any aspect.

Jaisingh Jadhav, on the other hand, is seen throughout as an investigative journalist with a trump card of his slave. His problem has nothing to do with how Sarita began to view him and their relationship but with his professional success and the dismissal from job. Nobody judges him by his private life, not even Sarita's uncle. Nobody wonders whether he is to 'blame' for his childlessness. She is hegemonically suppressed under the title of 'educated wife.' For her, the present position is a sense of 'reality' because she can't possibly think beyond that 'reality' in most areas of her life unless a woman like Kamala confronts her. Now Sarita realizes that she is powerless. It is apt to quote Jain's comments here. "Hi, Bhabhiji, I mean, an English, 'hi' to him, and a Marathi, 'hai' [*Alas*!] to you. This warrior against exploitation in country is exploiting you. He's made a drudge out of a horse-riding independent girl from a princely house. 'Hai,' 'hai' [*Theatrically to Jaisingh*] Shame on you! Hero of anti-exploitation campaigns makes slave of wife. . . . [*To Sarita*] Bye, lovely bonded labourer" (17).

Sarita is indeed an unpaid domestic bonded labourer. There is only one difference between Kamala and Sarita—Sarita is a labourer who is exploited by Jaisingh in the bond of marriage. Her bondage in the home prevents her to come out of those shackles and expose the male chauvinism of her husband at a press conference. Maya Pandit says: "Jaisingh is a pukka representation of the patriarchal ideology of what it means to be a husband" (69). Jaisingh turns out to be cruel not only towards Kamala but also towards his own wife Sarita. Kamala, to him, is only an object that helps him gain instant fame as a journalist. Sarita, to him, is, again, an object to be paraded as a wife at parties, to enhance his status as a successful journalist. In a sense, he is the typical Indian husband, who has no time to spare for his wife assuring her of his affection for her. Women are oppressed and exploited more than men in our society as it remains culturally patriarchal in spite of its having democracy.

In *Kamala,* if Jaisingh expects Kamala to appear at the press conference in her torn clothes and shabby state to suit his sense of the dramatic, he expects Sarita to submit to his desire for sex whether she wants it or not. While Sakharam beats up Champa when she refuses to have sex with him, the educated and socially committed Jaisingh calls Sarita a 'bitch.' Yet Sarita meekly accepts her subordinate position in the house, silently following every instruction to the last detail. It is only she who sees Jaisingh's selfish motives towards Kamala and realizes that there is not much difference between Kamala and herself.

When Jaisingh becomes a pawn in the political chess game played by his owner, Sheth Singhania, who dismisses him from the job, Kakasaheb says to Sarita, "This is the problem men face. The problem of achievement in the outside world." Shanta Gokhale points out that Tendulkar has not portrayed working women as working women and not highlighted their achievements in the outside world especially in their workplace: "We don't see Benare in her workplace; she is not 'tried' for her achievement in the outside world, that is, her commitment to and success in teaching children. She is tried for the relationship in her private life" (43).

In the play *Kanyadaan* also, though we are told that Jyoti is a working woman, the details about the nature of her job and workplace are not highlighted.

Even among working women journalists their works are invisible but seemingly unbreakable barrier like 'glass ceiling' as artificial barriers based on attitudinal or organizational biases preventing qualified women or ethnic minorities from advancing into upper management position and abstracting them. It is generally assumed that women abandon the executive track in order to spend more time with their families. Certainly, most executive officers of news organizations attribute the laws of women to family commitments.

Sarita, however, becomes aware of her real condition only when she converses with Kamala who asks her what price

Jaisingh has paid for her. To quote from one of the most pungent, ironic and historic episodes in the play:

> Kamala: Can I ask you something? You won't be angry?
> Sarita: No, Go On.
> Kamala: How much did he buy you for? (34)

Kamala's question opens Sarita's eyes suddenly and, for the first time, she finds no difference between herself and Kamala. She tells Kamala that Jaisingh bought her for seven hundred rupees. Kamala, though naïve, ignorant and illiterate, sympathizes with Sarita over her barrenness: "If you pay seven hundred and there are no children" (34). Sarita asks her: "How many children do you have, Kamala?" Kamala replies: "I will have as many as you want" (34). Kamala, thus, expresses her readiness to have children through Jaisingh to make the house a pleasant place to live in. She then proposes that she will do all the housework while Sarita will look after accounts and such 'sophisticated' things. She adds that each of them will share their master's bed half a month each. Sarita agrees to this. She realizes that she is also a slave like Kamala. When asked that Sarita's sudden recognition of her own enslaved condition with Kamala's question seems to be illogical, Tendulkar reacts in an interview with Gowri Ramnarayan: "The Indian woman is emerging from the traditional stronghold and finds things rather confusing. She has learnt that unless she asserts herself there is neither existence nor survival. In *Kamala* the wife's realization is the result of an accidental confrontation. The village woman's innocent question, 'For how much did he buy you?' is a revelation" (174).

By putting an innocent question in the mouth of so-called uncultured and illiterate woman, Tendulkar makes this incident unforgettable and historical in the entire Indian writing in English. Tendulkar's *Kamala* is a mighty mouthpiece in debunking the dominant prevailing patriarchal philosophical view that privileges reason and equals male thinking with rationality. Plato said that man is true humanity and that woman is deviation, woman is begotten male and mutilated male (Boss 326). Aristotle observed that heat is the fundamental principle of perfection in animals and women are colder than men and, therefore, less perfect than men. Sigmund Freud opined that woman's moral inferiority was the result of not so much a deficiency in intellectual development as in psychological development because women are less capable of acting on the basis of justice. Steven Goldenberg observed that patriarchy has a basis in biology; women are not equipped biologically to achieve equality with men in position of power and status. Besides, being making an attacker against these age-old notions, Tendulkar portrays Kamala as a woman who is in no way less than a man like Jaisingh, in the faculty of reason, intellect, observation and emotions. That she is portrayed in all these aspects more than him questions the gender discrimination in Indian society.

After his return from the Nari Niketan, Jaisingh asks his wife to go with him to a party. Sarita, defiant now, tells him that she does not want to accompany him there. Jaisingh, surprised at her defiance which is a sea change he notices in her, goes alone to the party. Kakasaheb, who has been away to the city, now comes in, and sees Sarita sitting, rather depressed, on the sofa and asks the reason for her depression. Here, Sarita refers to Jaisingh, her husband, by the term 'gentleman' underlining the fact that he has now become a stranger to her life. Sarita, like Nora in Ibsen's *A Doll's House,* has, thus, undergone a sea change, and now is entirely an independent and assertive woman who has finally discovered her real identity. His sheer self-centredness and hypocrisy give her the last impetus to leave. Jaisingh, on the other hand, is betrayed by his editor after all the credit he brought the Paper with his press conference. Sarita postpones her own decision about the future in order to give him the moral support he needs. She decides to lock up all her views about him for the time being. She is optimistic and affirmative that she will stop being a slave but not to stop being a compassionate human being. Nevertheless, she is not ready to change her opinion about marriage and husband-wife relationship:

> I'll go on feeling it. But at present I'm going to lock all that up in a corner of my mind and forget about it. But a day will come, Kakasaheb, when I will stop being a slave. . . . That day has to come. And I'll pay whatever price I have to pay for it. (52)

Kakasaheb is both fascinated and impressed by the quiet determination in her words. The play ends with Sarita, looking at the child-like face of the sleeping Jaisingh, remarking: "How innocent even the masters look when they're asleep" (52).

Tendulkar was criticized many times for his depiction of harsh realities of life without any sugar-coating and without suggesting any solution. In the contemporary Marathi drama, at least he has guts of showing raw violence faced by women in many forms. He was able to perceive the real state of women in the patriarchal society. Nevertheless, his exposing and exploration of women's problems paved the way for Marathi theatre to look at their problems with women's perspective. One thing is certain that whatever be their socio-economic background—Sakharam, Jaisingh, Ramakant, Prof. Damle—all have one thing in common—they see women as subject to be exploited, as possessions, not as individuals with feelings and desires of their own. The women have to limit themselves to the circle of restraint that confines them. According to differences in background—social, economic, educational—the circumference may be greater or lesser but the restraining circle is very much there!

Arundhati Banerjee in 'Introduction' makes a remark: "*Kamala* is an indictment of the success-oriented male-dominated society where women are often victims or stepping stones in men's achievements" (18). Obviously, women not only become stepping stones in the achievements of men who crave for success but also turn out to be guinea pigs in the hands of them. But Tendulkar's portrayal of Jaisingh to be another Kamala who is betrayed by Sheth Singhania can also be concluded that *Kamala* is an indictment of the business-oriented capital dominated society where men like Jaisingh becomes guinea pigs in the success of a capitalist.

Works Cited

Arundhati Banerjee. Introduction. *Five Plays* by Vijay Tendulkar. New Delhi: Oxford UP, 1992.

Boss, A. Judith. *Analyzing Moral Values*. California: Mountview Mayfield, 1992.

Christmas, Linda. "Chaps of Both Sexes? Women—Decision Makers in Newspapers: Do they make Difference?" *Women in Journalism*. London: BT Forum, 1997.

Gokhale, Vikram. "On Kamala." *Vijay Tendulkar's Plays: An Anthology of Recent Criticism*, ed. V.M. Madge. Delhi: Pencraft International, 2007.

Gokhale, Shanta. "Tendulkar on his own Terms." *Vijay Tendulkar's Plays*: *An Anthology of Recent Criticism*, ed. V. M. Madge.

H.M. Parshley. *The Second Sex*. Trans. New York: Penguin, 1972.

Heren, Louis. *The Power of the Press?* London: Orbis, 1985.

Pandit, Maya. "Representation of Family in Modern Marathi Plays: Tendulkar, Dalvi and Elkunchwar." *Vijay Tendulkar's Plays*: *An Anthology of Recent Criticism*, ed. V.M. Madge.

Plato, *The Republic*. Trans. Desmond Lee. New York: Penguin, 1974,

Ramnarayan, Gowri. "A New Myth of Sisyphus!" Vijay Tendulkar and Girish Karnad in Conversation with Gowri Ramnarayan. *The Hindu* folio on Theatre, Feb. 1998: 13.

Sonalkar, Sudhir. "Vijay Tendulkar and the Metaphor of Violence." *The Illustrated Weekly of India*, November, 20-26, 1983: 21.

Sonia, Bathla. *Women, Democracy and the Media Cultural and Political Presentations in the Indian Press*. New Delhi: Sage, 1988.

Tendulkar, Vijay. Interview, Gowri Ramnarayan. *Vijay Tendulkar's Plays: An Anthology of Recent Criticism*, ed. V.M. Madge.

Tendulkar, Vijay. Interview. *The Indian Express*, 27 March 1983, 5.

Tendulkar, Vijay. Afterword. *Kanyadaan*. Delhi: Oxford UP, 1996.

Conclusion

The study in the foregoing pages reveals that Tendulkar's plays are steeped in social realism reflecting his own experiences and the stark realities about life. His writing is marked with turbulences and controversies. He brings out the ugly side of the cultural deformity that is prevalent in our society. He is obsessed with exploring the human psyche through drama. His uncompromising depiction of human predicament and tensions with a tinge of social realism posits him as a unique playwright of the modern Marathi theatre.

Tendulkar was writing at a time when there were playwrights like Girish Karnad, Mahesh Elkunchwar, Mohan Rakesh and Badal Sircar. And together, they were creating a kind of Renaissance in Indian theatre—a golden period in modern Indian Theatre. He was like a pathfinder for the younger generations. He frankly accepts the reality of humanity. He does not want to manipulate himself and the human situation. In an interview he says: "Man is a complex phenomenon; any attempt at simplification through generalization would be foolish. I feel it also falsifies the picture. I wouldn't do that, it's an obsession with me to capture human behaviour, exclusive and ever-changing. At every stage, what I perceived has been reflected in my work. It's not that I am writing now on a conclusion reached long ago." (Ramnarayan 172)

Thus his plays acquire great authenticity. His craving for the preservation of human values posits him as a legend in the world of theatre. He is real and outspoken both in his plays and life. He is criticized for his failure of offering any solution to the problems of mankind out of his philosophy in his plays. He feels that the human situation is so complex that we can hardly suggest any practical solutions. It is not his pessimism, but it is his truthfulness. Therefore, if the issues raised in Tendulkar's plays continue to be relevant even today, it is the failure of our social system in general and the State in particular.

Today, we cannot say it with certitude that Tendulkar will be a celebrity of the Marathi drama scene. However, we can say this with assertiveness that Tendulkar has guided Marathi drama that seemed to have lost its proper track, and has kept leading it for over two decades. His place and importance in this respect shall remain unique in the history of Marathi drama. There may be controversies regarding his greatness, but his achievements are beyond question.

Tendulkar was a bold man. He was threatened several times by political and cultural thugs. His play *Sakharam Binder* was banned by the State Censor Board; another play named *Gidhade* too was performed without tickets as that too faced Censor hurdles. His play *Ghashiram Kotwal* faced so much political pressure. Some of the socialists like the late N.G. Gore too opposed the play. With the intervention of the then-Prime Minister, Late Smt. Indira Gandhi, Tendulkar won the case which he challenged in the court. After Gujarat genocide Tendulkar's audacious comment "If I had a pistol, I would shoot Narendra Modi" (Tendulkar 7) evoked mixed reactions, with Modi's supporters burning his effigies and others lauding him for the anti-Modi tirade. He voiced against the loss of freedom in the aftermath of the blasts in Mumbai in newspapers.

Tendulkar's personal tragedies made him thoughtful. He grew up in a Bombay Chawl where life was a continuous struggle every day. Born to lower middle class parents, favourite child Vijay grew up with a mute visual of his father threatening his mother. His father's principles were a hurdle for match-making for his daughter. His two uncles turned mad, and he found his missing brother, an alcoholic, dead in a ditch. A stint in journalism enhanced his sense of immediate, unvarnished reality, while the rambles at night made him witness desperate moments—a sex worker who plied her trade with a child under the cot, a sudden brawl where he saw a man decapitated by a cracked liquor bottle. Terrible blows like the long illness of a bed-ridden wife, the death of a son and daughter, his own mounting health problems, and financial hurdles could not destroy his love of life. He wrote: "I think I am, slowly but definitely accepting the fact that very little time is left for me to do what I like. I am not in a rush but want to have whatever time is left for myself, the mind asks for mobility, not of the body" (Ramnarayan 90)

Tendulkar's plays represent a perception of reality and the hierarchical power structure which is completely different from the established perception in the contemporary cultural texts. Tendulkar's dramas reflect conflict between tradition and modernity, conventions and unorthodoxy which symbolize social reality. His characters are replete with high individualism which is sensational in contemporary Marathi theatre. Tendulkar has convinced himself in particular and the theatre world and the people in general that he presents the cardinal philosophical problems of mankind through his plays. It shows his concern for human existence. The degradation of existence has affected the psycho-social nature of man which mirrors in his plays. Tendulkar's imagination is absorbed with the exploration of the real. And this exploration of the real demonstrates his extraordinary power of probing, analyzing and interpreting the moral and psychological states of his characters. He exposes the hypocrisies of contemporary society. Most of his plays, *The Vultures, Silence! The Court is in Session, Sakharam Binder, Ghashiram Kotwal, Kamala, Kanyadaan* and *Encounter in Umbugland* show his concern for modern man's anguish. These plays are a replica of Tendulkar's questioning and probing spirit, not only as a playwright but also as a human being.

Tendulkar has never played the role of a puppeteer and reduced his characters to dumb and lifeless puppets. He has portrayed his characters with their own voice and expression. Dialogue, in a play, Tendulkar says, is an important element; each one has a personal way of saying things; a strictly personal expression. A dialogue establishes the character as a living person and not a cardboard character or the mouthpiece of the playwright. The choice of words signifies the culture of the person, his or her region, profession and in short the whole background. The speech pattern likewise helps to particularize the character and to make it an individual rather than a type. He says the utilization of silence, as the structural aspect of a play can be as expressive as the dialogue or the words. He brilliantly uses the pauses, a device which enhances the power of the emoted word considerably.

Theatre which was Tendulkar's major concern led him to make newer and newer discoveries in the vast realm of the human mind which still defies all available theories and logic. Tendulkar says: "As a writer I feel fascinated by the violent exploited-exploiter relationship and obsessively delve deep into it instead of taking a position against it. That takes me to a point where I feel that this relationship is eternal, a fact of life however cruel, and will never end. Not that I relish this thought while it grips me but I cannot shake it off" (Tendulkar 147). His major plays reflect his social realism.

Tendulkar's *Silence! The Court is in Session* exposes the crooked relationship of power between husband and wife in married life, and also between married woman and unmarried woman. Benare's spirit of individualism makes her take a bold step of becoming pregnant with Prof. Damle without marriage. But Prof. Damle deceives her later, refusing to give his name to her child. Benare's defiance of the male-domination and her following trial explode the myth of motherhood as a sacred phenomenon and demonstrate how the biological phenomenon is deliberately highlighted in order to obtain control over woman's sexuality. The very fact of Mrs. Kashikar's collusion in the attack on Benare demonstrates how women internalize the dominance of men over themselves as a natural phenomenon. Tendulkar himself underscores the 'similarity' between *Silence! The Court is in Session* and his play *Gidhade:*

> In *Gidhade* it is the pack of human vultures pitched against a defenceless female character, the wife of Ramakant. In *Shantata!* it is Miss Benare against a pack of middle-class vultures. In *Gidhade*, Rajinikant, the bastard brother, suffers for the defenceless female in the play. In *Shantata* it was the character of Samant who did it for the psychologically-mauled Miss Benare (Bandyopadhyay xlix).

Silence! The Court is in Session establishes that the police and judiciary are after all the products of the same patriarchal system that subordinates women. Their attitudes to the victims as well as the perpetrators of violence are shaped by patriarchal beliefs. Ultimately, it is only a strong women's movement that can put the State machinery into action, change deep-rooted social attitudes and provide a safe space for victims.

Sakharam Binder delineates the political meaning of the family in which again women are the victims. The playwright exposes sex and violence of the lower class which are part and parcel of their life. The play exposes the double standards of men that patriarchy facilitates. *Sakharam Binder* also conveys a message that the institution of marriage must be saved for the survival of social stability and harmony.

Sakharam, who is a book-binder, does not believe in the institution of marriage and arranges for live-in relationships with single women. His relationship with Laxmi shows tendencies of being religious and domesticated. After Champa's arrival in his house, he is transformed into a sensuous, lewd, drunkard with thoughts only of sexual enjoyment. But he comes to know that Champa has also developed illicit contact with Dawood, his friend. Unable to bear this, his masculinity is badly hurt. Hence, in his anger, he kills Champa. However, the play exposes the greater hypocrisy in man-woman relationships in the matrix of the institution of marriage which poses a threat to the institution.

His play *Kanyadaan* is about an inter-caste marriage which exposes caste politics that take place in India. Tendulkar has focused on a problem that there is no bridge between the various sections of society, and that the attempt to overcome a taboo often leads to greater pitfalls. The play underscores the naiveté and hypocrisy of ideological parents. Nath Devlalikar and Seva are Brahmin couple actively working for a political party. Their daughter Jyoti decides to marry a dalit boy, a poet, Arun Athawale much against her mother's repeated warnings. After she has read Arun's autobiography which is packed with lies, Jyoti feels sympathetic towards Arun and thinks that she can do anything for Arun. However, Nath fully supports his daughter in this aspect and he is rather excited and ecstatic for he thinks his ideological dream is going to be realized. In this way he crucifies his own daughter, Jyoti for his ideological experiment. As a result, her marriage becomes a nightmare to her within no time as Arun's real form of character is unveiled. Arun is not only a drunkard but also a wife-beater, manipulator and blackmailer. In fact he marries Jyoti with the cunning motive of taking revenge against upper class who treated his ancestors badly. At the end Jyoti realizes her father's hypocrisy and cries out whether his ideology, name and fame are more important to him than his daughter's life. The play concludes with Jyoti's decision of going back to her husband and not to see her parents ever. The play also exposes the oppression, exploitation and humiliation of women by their fathers and husbands in a patriarchal society. It is the best example in a situation where a man can use a woman to suit his purpose.

Tendulkar's famous play *Ghashiram Kotwal* deals with power politics in which once again women are exploited. The play has been presented through music, dance and chorus. The play is based on a historical incident taken from the life of Balaji Janardan Bhanu Peshwas' Phadnavis of Poona. He was a shrewd politician who succeeded in keeping Britishers away from the Maratha empire. He was hero worshipped by the people. But Tendulkar has chosen a shady side of his character in which he made Ghashiram Savaldas the Kotwal of Poona in exchange for his daughter, Lalita Gauri.

Ghashiram is a Brahmin from Kannauj and comes to Poona for a livelihood. But the Brahmins of Poona insult him and charge him with a theft. The innocent Ghashiram is punished for no fault of his. He is raged with revenge against those Brahmins. To attain power he prepares to sacrifice his innocent daughter to the lust of old Nana. Ghashiram becomes Kotwal of Poona and turns to his tormentors and becomes a terror. After losing interest in Gauri, Nana gets rid of her. Actually, Nana's intention in making Ghashiram a Kotwal is to remove him from his way. For this he uses Poona's Brahmins who think Ghashiram an outsider. At the end, Nana succeeds in his wicked plan and Ghashiram is murdered at the hands of people who are badly provoked by Nana. Thus, the play succeeds in presenting political power and importantly deals with universal human behaviour and weaknesses.

Kamala is a story of a sensational journalist Jaisingh Jadhav, who is self-centred and egotist. He buys an innocent woman Kamala in a flesh market and presents her in a press conference to prove the existence of flesh trade. It also presents the suppression of an educated woman Sarita who realizes her position later through Kamala. In a country like India there is no difference between a tribal woman and an educated woman: both are suppressed in a male chauvinistic society.

The play also exposes the negligible value of woman as a commodity in the modern world. Kamala is a tribal, innocent and illiterate; Sarita, an educated urban woman who is a house wife, both are portrayed as commodities in the market which can be sold off for cash. The play exposes not only the role of State machinery in such a heinous crime of women trafficking but also the collusion of the Press with the State as an ideological apparatus of power to show unequal relations in society. It also satirizes sensational journalism—the kind practised by self-seeking journalists like Jaisingh Jadhav who sacrifices human values in the name of humanity itself.

Tendulkar's plays are open to diverse interpretations and cannot be tied down to a single line of thinking. Therefore, the question whether Tendulkar writes for life's sake or for art's sake will not arise. Though he seems to favour socialism, his plays do not reflect this ideology. He is a playwright of humanism who paints it in his plays in garish colours. He is not an escapist. Tendulkar says: "If escapism is your way of living then you will fail to see the truth" (Raghunath).

The greater quality which Tendulkar can claim as a creative writer and dramatist is the ability to simultaneously involve and distance himself from his creation. This endows his works with infinite subtlety. As Arundhati Banerjee remarks: "none of his creations are ever simplistic—like his genius they too have the same prismatic quality of giving forth new meanings as one turns them around in the light of one's understanding" (584).

All the five plays taken for study here have a direct, one-to-one reflection of social reality. In all these plays, Tendulkar portrays the different aspects of the human character and highlights the complexity of human relationships. Moreover, in all of them, women play significant or key roles in the plot. All the works contain a hidden critique of modern Indian society, mostly middle-class and lower middle-class, from different angles.

Vijay Tendulkar's multi-faceted creative genius continued to experiment and explore the potentials of the dramatic genre—his primary area of creation until his death. He was a man of human nature and a dramatist of social realism of not only modern Marathi theatre but also modern Indian drama.

Works Cited

Banerjee, Arundhati. Introduction. *Five Plays* by Vijay Tendulkar. New Delhi: Oxford University Press, 1992.

Raghunath, Rama. "Conversation with Vijay Tendulkar." //html. www. Vijay Tendulkar.google.com.html.

Tendulkar, Vijay. "Vijay Tendulkar in Conversation with Gowri Ramnarayan." *Vijay Tendulkar's Plays: An Anthology of Recent Criticism*, ed. V.M. Madge. Delhi: Pencraft International, 2007.

Ramnarayan, Gowri. "Writing for Life." *Front Line* 20 June 2008: 91.

Tendulkar, Vijay. "The Man Wanted to Shoot Modi." *Times of India* 19 May 2005: 7.

Bibliography

Primary Sources

Tendulkar, Vijay. *Collected Plays in Translation.* New Delhi: Oxford UP, 2003. This book contains: *Encounter in Umbugland.* Trans. Priya Adarkar; *Ghashiram Kotwal.* Trans. Jayant Karve and Eleanor Zelliot; *Kamala*. Trans. Priya Adarkar; *Kanyadaan*. Trans. Gowri Ramnarayan; *Sakharam Binder.* Trans. Kumud Mehta and Shanta Gokhale; *Silence! The Court is in Session.* Trans. Priya Adarkar; *The Vultures*. Trans. Priya Adarkar; *A Friend's Story.* Trans. Gowri Ramnarayan.

_____. *Muslim and I.* (The Theatre and I). Bombay: Dimple Publications, 1997.

_____. *His Fifth Woman.* Trans. Balwant Bhaneja, Oxford University Press, New Delhi, 2006.

_____. *The Cyclist.* Trans. Balwant Bhaneja. New Delhi: Oxford University Press, 2006.

_____. *View from the Balcony.* New Delhi: Katha Vilasam, 2001.

Tendulkar, Vijay. *Criminals and Killers: A Personal View.* New Delhi: Sahitya Akademi, 2002.

Interviews

Kakar, Sudhir. "Marriage: War between the Sexes." *The Indian Express. Weekend Magazine* 7 June 1987: 1+.

Kameswari, Jandhyala. "At His Majesty's Pleasure." *The Indian Express, Weekend Magazine,* 25 Nov. 1989: 3+.

K.K. Birla Foundation's "Third Saraswati Samman Award Note." *Kanyadaan*. Mumbai: Popular Prakashan, 1994: xv.

Palekar, Amol. "To Preserve a Theatre Tradition." By Pinglay. *The Hindu*, folio on theatre, 30 Oct. 1998: 5+.

Pandey, Sudhakar and Freya Barua, ed. "Casanova as the Saviour: A Study of Vijay Tendulkar's *Sakharam Binder.*" *New Directions in Indian Drama*. New Delhi: Prestige, 1994. 33-40.

"Prevention of Prostitution." *League of Nations Report.* Geneva: 1943:8.

Tendulkar, Vijay. “A Rich Tapestry of Women Stories.” *The Hindu* folio on Theatre 6 Nov. 2005: 5.

Tendulkar, Vijay. “*Natak Ani Mee.*” Interview with Shirish Pai, Priya Tendulkar. Thane: Dimple Publications. 1997: 188.

Tendulkar, Vijay. “The Play is the Thing.” Sri Ram Memorial Lecture. New Delhi: Sri Ram Centre for Performing Arts, 1997: xiii.

Tendulkar, Vijay. “Vijay Tendulkar: When Writing is Life Itself.” Interview with K. Kannan. *The Hindu* 16 Sept. 2001: 54+.

Tendulkar, Vijay. “A New Myth of Sisyphus!” Vijay Tendulkar and Girish Karnad in Conversation with Ramnarayan. *The Hindu*, folio on theatre. Feb. 1998: 16+.

Tendulkar, Vijay. “Afterword.” *Kanyadaan.* Delhi: Oxford University Press, 1996: 71.

Tendulkar, Vijay. “Drama: The Most Difficult, But the Most Powerful Medium.” *Interviews with Indian Writers. New World Literature Series* B-18-280.

Tendulkar, Vijay. Interview. *India Today* Dec. 16-31, 1980: 157.

Tendulkar, Vijay. “No Ideology.” Interview. *India Today,* June 16-30, 1980: 110+.

Tendulkar, Vijay. “Writing for Life.” *Frontline*, June 7-20, 2008: 86.

Tendulkar, Vijay and Satyadev Dubey. “Dialogue-Offstage.” *Gentleman,* Sep. 1983: 62+.

Secondary Sources

(A) Books

Ambedkar, Baba Saheb. *Writings and Speeches.* Vol. 3 Bombay: Government of Maharashtra, 1987.

Awasthi, Suresh. *Drama, the Gift of Gods: Culture, Performance, and Communication in India.* Tokyo: ILCAA, 1983.

Beauvoir, Simone de. *The Second Sex.* England: Penguin, 1972.

Benegal, Shyam. *A Panorama of Theatre in India.* Bombay: Popular Prakashan (for) Indian Council for Cultural Relations, 1967.

Bharucha, Rustom. *Rehearsals of Revolution: The Political Theatre of Bengal.* Honolulu: University of Hawaii Press, 1983.

Blum, Gerald S. *Psychoanalytical Theories of Personality.* New York: McGraw Hill, 1953.

Campbell, Joseph. *The Masks of God.* 3 Vols. Harmondsworth: Penguin, 1976.

Chambers, Debroah et.al. *Women and Journalism.* London: Routledge, 2004.

Chowdary, Shoma and Gita Rajan, ed. *Vijay Tendulkar.* New Delhi: Kathavilasam, 2001.

Das, S.K. *A History of Indian Literature.* Vol. 9. New Delhi: Sahitya Akademi, 1995.

_____, ed. *Modern Indian Drama: An Anthology.* New Delhi: Sahitya Akademi, 2000.

Dasgupta, Hemendranath. *The Indian Stage.* 4 Vols. Calcutta: Metropolitan Printing and Publishing House, 1944.

Dass, Veena Noble. *Modern Indian Drama in English Translation.* Hyderabad: 1988.

Dharan, N.S. *The Plays of Vijay Tendulkar.* New Delhi: Creative, 1999.

Dharwadkar, Aparna Bhargava. *Theatre of Independence Drama: Theory and Urban Performance in India since 1947.* New Delhi: Oxford UP, 2005.

Doniger, Wendy and Brian K. Smith, trans. *The Laws of Manu.* London: Penguin, 1991.

Dumont, Louis, ed. *Homo Hierarchicus: The Caste System and its Implications.* Chicago: University of Chicago Press, Rev. 1980.

Freud, Sigmund. *New Introductory Lectures on Psychoanalysis.* London: OUP, 1986.

Gai, S.K. *Women and Media Decision Making: The Invisible Barriers.* New Delhi: Sterling, 1987.

Gandhi, M.K. *India of My Dream.* Comp. R.K. Prabhu. Ahmedabad: Navajivan, 1962.

Karnad, Girish and Rajinder Paul, ed. *Contemporary Indian Theatre: Interviews with Playwrights and Directors.* New Delhi: Sangeet Natak Akademi, 1989.

Gokhale, Shanta. *Playwright at the Centre: Marathi Drama from 1843 to the Present.* Calcutta: Seagull, 2000.

Gramsci, A. *Selections from the Prison Notebook.* London: Lawrence and Wishart, 1971.

Harris, Thomas, A. *I'm OK—You're OK.* New Delhi: Sterling, 1979.

Iyengar, Srinivas. *Indian Writing in English.* (5th edition). New Delhi: Sterling, 1985.

Kapadia, K.M. *Marriage and Family in India.* Bombay: Bhacker, 1975.

Karnad, Girish. *In Search of a Theatre in Contemporary India: Essays on the Use of Tradition*, ed. Karla Borden. Delhi: Oxford University Press, 1989.

Levi, Sylvain. *The Theatre of India.* 2 Vols. Trans. Narayan Mukherji. Calcutta: Writer's Workshop, 1978.

Livingstone, Sonia. *Young People and New Media.* New Delhi: Sage, 2002.

Madge, V.M., ed. *Vijay Tendulkar's Plays: An Anthology of Recent Criticism.* Delhi: Pencraft International, 2007.

Martha, A. Fineman and Martha, T. Mc Cluskey, ed. *Feminism, Media and the Law.* New York: Oxford UP, 1997.

Mies, M. *Patriarchy and Accumulation on a World Scale.* London: Zed, 1986.

Mill, James. *The History of British India.* 6 Vols. London: Baldwin, 1820.

_____. *Program for Urubhangam.* Mysore: Dhvanyaloka, 1987.

Mynemi, S.R. *Women and Law.* Hyderabad: Asia Law House, 2005.

_____.*Jurisprudence (Legal Theory).* Hyderabad: Asian Law House, 2004.

Naik, M.K. *Critical Essays on Indian Writing in English.* Dharwad: Karnataka University, 1972.

_____.*History of Indian English Literature.* New Delhi: Sahitya Akademi, 1982.

Nelson, C. and L. Gyossberg, ed. *Marxism and the Interpretation of Culture.* London: Macmillan Education, 1988.

Pandey, Sudhakar and Freya Barua, ed. *New Directions in Indian Drama.* New Delhi: Prestige, 1994.

_____ and Freya Taraporewala, ed. *Contemporary Indian Drama.* New Delhi: Prestige, 1990.

Ramabai, Pandita. *The High Caste Hindu Woman.* Bombay: Maharashtra State Board of Literature and Culture, 1981.

Rayan R, Reiter, ed. *Towards an Anthropology of Women.* London: Monthly Review Press, 1975.

Reginald, Edward. *The Folklore of Bombay.* Bombay: Oxford UP, 1924.

Rosaldo, M.Z. and L. Lamphere, ed. *Woman, Culture and Society: A Theoretical Overview.* California: Stanford University Press, 1974.

Said, Edward M. *Orientalism.* New York: Vintage, 1979.

Sarat Babu, Manchi. *Vijay Tendulkar's Ghashiram Kotwal: A Reader's Companion.* New Delhi: Asia Book Club, 2003.

_____.*Indian Drama Today: A Study in the Theme of Cultural Deformity.* London: Sangam, 1997.

Sarkar, Lotika and Sivaramayya, ed. *Women and Law: Contemporary Problems.* New Delhi: Vikas, 1994.

Scott, A.C. *The Theatre in Asia.* London: Weiderfelt and Nicolson, 1977.

Sethi, Rumina. *Myths of the Nation: National Identity and Literary Representation.* Oxford: Clarendon Press, 1999.

Sircar, Badal. *Bakti Itihas.* Trans. Nemichandra Jain. Delhi: Akshar Prakashan, 1969.

_____. *The Changing Languages of Theatre.* New Delhi: Indian Council for Cultural Relations, 1982.

_____. *The Third Theatre.* Calcutta: Badal Sircar, 1978.

_____. *Voyages in the Theatre.* Shri Ram Memorial Lectures. No.4. New Delhi: Shri Ram Centre for Performing Arts, 1993.

Sukumar, M.A.K. *The Last Plays of Shakespeare: A Study.* Tirupati: Sri Venkateshwara University, 2001.

Tanvir, Habib. *Charandas Chor.* New Delhi: Pustakayan, 1997.

Van Erven, Eugene. *Radical People's Theatre.* Bloomington: Indian University Press, 1988.

Varad, Pande M.L. and Sunil Subhedar et.al. *The Critique of Indian Theatre.* Delhi: Unique, 1981.

Vatsyayan, Kapila. *Traditional Indian Theatre: Multiple Streams.* New Delhi: National Book Trust, 1980.

Wells, Henry W. *The Classical Drama of India: Studies in its Values for the Literature and Theatre of the World.* New York: Asia, 1963.

Williams, R. *Keywords: A Vocabulary of Culture and Society.* New York: Oxford UP, 1976.

Yarrow, Ralph. *Indian Theatre: Theatre of Origin, Theatre of Freedom.* Richmond, UK: Curzon Press, 2001.

(B) Articles

Abrams, Tevia. "Folk Theatre in Maharashtrian Social Development Programme." *Educational Theatre Journal* 27-3 (Oct. 1975): 395-407.

Bhalla, Neela. "*Ghashiram Kotwal*: Text and Sub-text." *Vijay Tendulkar's Plays: An Anthologhy of Recent Criticism*, ed. V.M. Madge. Delhi: Pencraft International, 2007: 130-42.

Christmas, Linda. "Chaps of Both Sexes? Women-Decision-Makers in Newspapers: Do they make Difference?" *Women in Journalism.* London: BT Forum: 213.

Desai, H. Ashok. "Censorship and *Sakharam Binder*." Preface to *Sakharam Binder. Enact* (1987): 7-11.

Gokhale, Shanta. "Tendulkar on his own Terms." in Madge. 30-61.

Gokhale, Vikram. "On Kamala." in Madge. 151-52.

Havenurkar, Jyoti. "Levity and Seriousness in *Silence! The Court is in Session*," in Madge. 98-105.

Karnad, Girish. "Author's Introduction." *Nagamandala, Tughlaq, Hayavadana*. Delhi: Oxford UP, 1994: 15.

Limaye R. Mohan. "The Archetypal Identity of Laxmi in *Sakharam Binder*." *Modern Asian Studies* 121 (1978): 140-41.

Nadkarni, Dyaneshwar. "*Ghashiram Kotwal*." *Enact* (Jan.-Feb. 1973): 73-74.

_____. "*Contemporary Marathi Theatre*," in Pandey and Taraporewala, 9-12.

Nadkarni, Dyaneshwar. "The Case of Sakharam Binder." *Enact*. 66 (June 1972): 64-65.

Naik. "Ghashiram Kotwal Remains Controversial." *The Times of India* 20 June, 2000: 29+.

Nishikant. Mirajkar. D. "Two Recent Plays of Vijay Tendulkar," in Pandey and Barua, 37-41

Pandit, Maya. "Representation of Family in Modern Marathi Plays: Tendulkar, Dalvi and Elkunchwar," in Madge, 62-79.

Sonalkar, Sudhir. "Vijay Tendulkar and the Metaphor of Violence." *The Illustrated Weekly of India*, 18-24 Nov, 1993: 20-24.

Tapas, Vijay. "*Tendulkar: The Number Two Anti-Dalit*." *Adhikar Raksha*. Bulletin of the Committee for Protection of Democratic Rights, Bombay (Jan.-June 1983): 64.

Tendulkar, Vijay. "I am against Sensational Journalism." *The Sunday Observer*, Oct. 1982: 6+.

_____. "Introduction." *Ghashiram Kotwal*. Calcutta: Seagull, 1984: ix.

_____. "Writers Note." *Ghashiram Kotwal*. Hindi Trans. Vasant Deo. New Delhi: Radha Krishnan, 1983: 8.

Thankamma, Catherine. "Woman that Patriarchy Created: The Plays of Vijay Tendulkar, Mahesh Dattani and Mahasweta Devi," in Magde, 80-87.

Valdez Edna and Kim Wright. "What Men Can Learn from Women and Leadership." *Together* (Oct.-Dec. 1991): 14.

Zoonam, Van L. "A Tyranny of Intimacy: Women, Femininity and Television News." *Communication and Citizenship*, ed. P. Dahlgren and C. Sparks. London: Routledge, 1991. 106+.

Web Sources

Bhaneja, Balwant. Interview, "Vijay Tendulkar (1928-2008)." http://www.hotreview.org/articles/vijaytendulkar.htm

Rajyadhyaksha, Mukta. Interview. Vijay Tendulkar (28th Oct. 2009). http://passionforcinema.com/a-conversation-with-sir-vijay_tendulkar/

Peter Joseph, John S. "The Playwright as a Social Critic: A Critical Study of Vijay Tendulkar's *Silence! The Court is in Session.*" 15 October, 2009. http://www.google.com/

Ramnarayan, Gowri. "Response to Conversation with Sir Vijay Tendulkar." www.Vijay Tendulkar Google Search (20 Dec. 2006).

Rama, Raghunath. "Vijay Tendulkar: Voice of Social Stage is Dead." //www.*The Telegraph* (Tuesday, 20 May 2008).

Ayachit, Santosh. "We can never understand Vijay Tendulkar." //html.www.vijaytendulkar.google search.com.tm

Carolyn, M. Byerly and Karen Ross. "Woman and Media: A Critical Introduction." Blackwell, Howard University. http://www.media and woman.org

Deepa, Gahlat. "*Tendulkar: The World Is His Stage.*" //www.spectrum. The Tribune (Sunday Oct., 2004).

Katju, Markandey. "Ideal and Reality: Media's Role in India." *The Hindu*, Aug. 19, 2008.

Videos from Youtube:

- Tendulkar And Violence Then and Now—Marathi Documentary https://www.youtube.com/watch?v=Jv475KO5jfw
- *Ghashiram Kotwal*-Marathi Natak https://www.youtube.com/watch?v=4_Fc_e0L66I
- *Silence! The Court is in Session* https://www.youtube.com/user/sibinm?feature=watch
- *Kamla* (1984) movie directed by Jag Mundhra with Shabana Azmi, Deepti Naval and Marc Zuber https://www.youtube.com/movie?v=r6AJ8gAzejA&feature=mv_sr
- Vijay Tendulkar's Literary Journey by NDTV https://www.youtube.com/watch?v=-TsjvzHyAA4

APPENDIX

Chronology of Tendulkar's Life

1928: Vijay Tendulkar is born.
1944: Starts his first job in a press.
1948: Works as Sub-Editor in *Navbharat*.
1950: Works as an Executive Editor of *Vasudha* and *Dipawali*.
1951: Enters Bharatiya Vidya Bhavan.
1956: The second play *Shrimant* (*The Rich*) wins the award of Maharashtra State Government.
1959: Becomes the Vice Chairman of Rangayan.
1961: Works as Sub-Editor in P.K. Atre's popular newspaper *Maratha*.
1967: Becomes the PRO of Chaugule Industries. Writes columns for *Manus* and *Maharashtra Times*.
1968: Works as Co-Editor of *Loksatta*.
1969: A collection of one act plays *Ajagar Ani Gandharva* (*The Python and the Gandharva*) wins Maharashtra State Government Award.
1970: *Silence! The Court is in Session* awarded the Kamaladevi Chattopadhyaya Prize. Becomes a member of New Bombay Planning Team.
1971: Wins Sangeet Natak Akademi Award. Becomes the President of *Avishkar*
1973: The Miscellany *Kovali Unhe* wins the State Government Award.
1976: Becomes the President of Granthali.
1977: The Hindi film *Manthan* wins National Award for the best film. Becomes a member of the General Council of Musical Drama Academy.
1978: Becomes a Member of the General Council. Sahitya Akademi, New Delhi. Works as Guest Lecturer at Tata Institute of Social Studies.
1979: Becomes Vice Chairman of the National School of Drama.
1980: The Film *Akrosh* wins Filmfare award for the best screenplay and dialogue.
1983: Awarded Padma Bhushan.

1986: Becomes emeritus produced in Akashwani and Doordarshan.
1988: Becomes a Member of National Integration Committee.
1991: Receives Kalidas Award. Honoured by the Maharashtra State Government.
1992: Drama Festival of his play in memory of Arvind Deshpande.
1999: Wins Janasthan Award and Maharashtra Gaurav Puraskar
2005: Drama Festival of his plays organized by Amole Palekar.
2008: Passes away in Mumbai on 19 May.